# FOWNHOPE REMEMBERED

## Change in a Herefordshire Village 1919-2000

## CONTENTS

## Edited by David M Clark

## FOWNHOPE LOCAL HISTORY GROUP

with financial support from
The Local Heritage Initiative

*Fownhope Remembered*
© Fownhope Local History Group, 2007

ISBN 978-0-9557867-0-9

ISBN-13:  978-0-9557867-0-9

British Library Cataloguing in Publication Data available

Editor:  David M Clark

Fownhope Local History Group
c/o 2 Ringfield Drive Fownhope, HR1 4PR

Printed by Orphans Press, Leominster, HR6 0LD

*Front cover illustrations:*
Stony Row and Tump Cottage 1907    *Vera E Biggs*
Fred Powell's milk round c1930    *Doris Bond*
WI Jubilee 1984    *Pip Leyman*
Old School before 1956    *Pip Leyman*

Supported by
The National Lottery®
through the Heritage Lottery Fund

Heritage
Lottery Fund

# OUR THANKS to

**ORAL INTERVIEWS** Denzil Biggs, Margaret Biggs, Vera E Biggs, Doris Bond, Derrick Brown, Sue Clifford, Dorothy Crowe, Joan Davies, Dennis Evans, Dora Grant, Derek Griffiths, John Hardwick, Carol Hart, Jennifer Higham, Joan Hill, Jean Hook, Pat Homan, Dolly & John Hoyes, Jill & Ray Howard Jones, John T Jones Sen, Pip Leyman, Keith Mason, Norma Massey, May Meredith, John Newman, Phil Paton, Jean Phillips, Ted Pocknell, Rose Pullen, Mary & Patrick Ramage, Harry Robbins, Judith Rogers, Noel Taylor, Bill Taylor, Irene Thomas, Lilian Thomas, Melvyn Wargen, John Westley, Nora Whittall, Gareth Williams, Mabel & Michael Williams, Phyllis Yarranton.

**ORAL INTERVIEWERS** Pam & Derek Colley, Madge Daines, Mandy Dees, Rachael Best, Janet & Ian Jones, David V Clarke, John Gill, David & Margaret Clark *(co-ordinator)*

**RESEARCH** *in city, cathedral & Birmingham libraries, Hereford & Worcester record offices, National Archive at Kew, websites.*
Ian & Janet Jones, Mandy Dees, David V Clarke, Pam Colley, Michael Best, Neenie Cope *(nee* Malkin), David Lovelace, Margaret & David M Clark *(convenor).*

**PHOTOS & DOCUMENTS** Michael Andrews, Joan Banks, Michael & Rachael Best, Denzil Biggs, Lionel & Margaret Biggs, Vera E Biggs, Vera M Biggs, Doris Bond, David & Jean Boothman, Bowls Club, British Legion, Brockhampton Cricket Club, Derrick & Ann Brown, Rosemary Brown, Clare Buck, Pam Burke, David & Anna Campion, Brian Chamberlain, David & Margaret Clark, Rev David Clarke, Sue & Austyn Clifford, Derek & Pam Colley, Neenie Cope, Peter & Madge Daines, Rev Jane Davies, Joyce Davies, Rev Mandy Dees, Shelagh Donnelly, Forestry Commission, John Gill, Sue & Kevin Gough, Dora Grant, Ken & Ann Gray, Peter & Shirley Green, Derek Griffiths, John Hardwick, Herefordshire Council, Hereford Record Office, Jill & Ray Howard Jones, Heather Hurley. Louisa Hyde, John Jones snr, John T. Jones, Tony & Avril Jones, Dennis Lacey, W Lewis, Pip Leyman, David Lovelace / Landscapes of Wye project, Margot Miller, Scott Morrall, Anne Morris, Liv Moss, Herefordshire Nature Trust, John Newman, Fownhope Parish Council, Robin Peers, Play Group, Tom Plumley, Gerald Powell, Rev Will Pridie, Barbara Pritchard, Rosie Pullen, Mary & Dr Patrick Ramage, Margret & Geoffrey Rolls, Clarence Sayce, Morrison Sellars, Beryl Snape *(née* Lloyd), Jeremy Soulsby, St Mary's School, Sky Library, Sue Stannard, Irene Thomas, Lilian Thomas, Townsend family, Vernon Thompson, Connie Townsend, Roy Wargen, Alfred Watkins, Kath Watkins, Christopher Whitmey, Maxine Williams, Michael Williams, Wye Valley AONB.

**PHOTOGRAPHERS** *record of every building in 2006* Peter Daines, Sue Clifford, Sue Gough, Ann Corby, David V Clarke, Margaret & David M Clark.

**COMMITTEE** *2005-7* Rev Mandy Dees (chair), Rachael & Michael Best, David & Margaret Clark, Rev David V Clarke, Sue Clifford, Pam Colley, Ann Corby, Sue Gough, Ian & Janet Jones, Margot Miller (2005).

# FOWNHOPE REMEMBERED

*Dedicated to all the people who through their lives and actions
have helped to shape the modern community we know today*

The *Fownhope Local History Group* was set up in early 2005 and was fortunate
to get generous funding from the *Local Heritage Initiative* to record Fownhope
'within living memory'. This book is a flavour of what we have collected.
We have drawn on the recordings of 50 interviews, copies of photographs,
and extracts from local papers, club, business records, and documents from
record offices and libraries. It is remarkable how much has been kept but
sadly some records have been lost including the early parish magazines
and parish council minutes.

*Wilf Chignell conducting the village orchestra c 1952*

Where possible we have brought the story up to the present day, but we
have left some aspects of the last decade for a future generation to record.
Much has been displayed at our five exhibitions which attracted more than
a thousand visitors.

We have created a permanent 'archive' of exhibition and research material,
and hope to produce more books to record the story of everyday life in the
years before 1919 in this fascinating Herefordshire village. History matters
– pass it on.

*David M Clark, Editor*
*Fownhope, December 2007*

# FOWNHOPE IN 1919

Fownhope was one of Herefordshire's larger villages. The church was considered one of the county's premier churches in Norman times. The wide-spread parish had included two detached chapelries of Fawley and Strangford until the 1880s. There were a range of landowners including many small owners. Property changed hands freely, bringing in many newcomers. The village had thrived in the 18th and early 19th centuries when its brewery, tanyards and lime kilns served a very wide area of the county, albeit at the mercy of the capricious river trade. The village had had a school and doctor from the mid 18th century, and the *Amicable Society,* founded in 1791, was one of the first.

*Main road & Tump Cottage about 1907*                              *Vera E Biggs*

But by 1919 Fownhope was in decline. The population (*719 in the 1921 census*) had fallen by 22% since 1881. Families had drifted away to better prospects in the towns or overseas. Twenty homes were empty. Twelve men had died in action in the war – one from every 15 households. What had once been a pioneering village could only look on as neighbours in the cathedral city of Hereford, seven miles away, enjoyed electricity, mains water, drains, motorised buses and a rail service. Fownhope folk had to carry water some distance from wells. They had no electricity, sewers or refuse collection. Housing conditions were unsanitary, though the village still had a doctor. There was a horse-driven carrier to town twice a week, and some crossed the toll bridge to Holme Lacy station.

Morney Cottage water colour *undated*                    *J Soulsby*

The largest landowners, the Lechmere family, were in retreat. The Lord of the Manor, absentee owners of Haugh Wood, had no day-to-day involvement with the village. The brewery and other industries were long gone. The village relied on work on the farms, the woods, a range of shops and trades, and others in service. The School built in 1868, with the four pubs, shops, St Mary's Church, and the two chapels, provided focal points for community life. The *Heart of Oak Society* provided medical and unemployment benefits for many of the men, and had organised the annual *Club Walk* and dinner before the war, an event which rivalled the village *Flower Show*. There were no sports field or sports clubs. Much was about to change.

Tympanum west wall of Church c 1919          *Alfred Watkins*

6

# POPULATION CHANGE

Fownhope's population remained static through the 1920s and 30s but fell by 8% in the post-war period to 662 in the 1951 census, though there were 10 more occupied homes.

There was a slight increase in population between 1951 and 1961, due to the long-awaited development of Court Orchard, followed by a rapid rise after the arrival of mains water and sewerage. Fownhope's population reached 1073 in the 1981 census – almost as many as it had been in the heyday of 1871.

| 1921 | 1931 | 1951 | 1961 | 1971 | 1981 |
|------|------|------|------|------|------|
| 719 | 723 | 662 | 724 | 857 | 1073 |

Boundary changes in 1986 transferred 130 people into Mordiford parish but more development brought a 25% increase in houses by 2001, though the population remained stable as households continued to contract in line with the national trend.

| | 1981 | 1991 | 2001 |
|---|------|------|------|
| Population | 945 | 895 | 959 |
| Dwellings | 349 | 382 | 436 |

Development brought other changes. Only one in five residents was employed in professional and managerial jobs at the time of the 1971 census. By 2001 the proportion had doubled to 42%, compared to the county average of 34%. In 1971 there were 120 people with qualifications to A level or above, but this had also doubled to 228 in 2001, with 180 recorded having degrees or their equivalent.

# HOUSING CONDITIONS

Housing conditions in the 1920s compared unfavourably with the towns. The *District Medical Officer of Health* reported in 1935 that more than a third of the 190 inhabited houses in Fownhope were seriously defective or in need of repair, more than any other local parish. The first improvement grant was given to Mr Clay of Brockhampton for work on Capler Wood Cottage in 1937.

*Fern Cottage 1952 – 'plaster off the wall, no water, lots of mice – they used to stand up on their back legs looking at you!'*
*Phil Paton talking to Pam Colley & Madge Daines 2006*

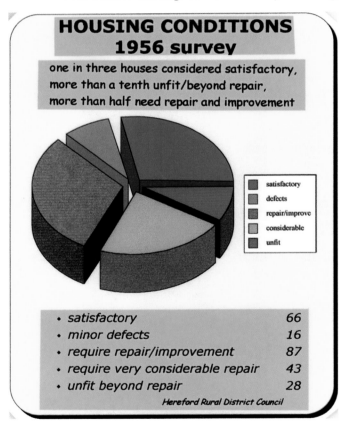

**HOUSING CONDITIONS 1956 survey**

one in three houses considered satisfactory,
more than a tenth unfit/beyond repair,
more than half need repair and improvement

- satisfactory
- defects
- repair/improve
- considerable
- unfit

| | |
|---|---|
| • satisfactory | 66 |
| • minor defects | 16 |
| • require repair/improvement | 87 |
| • require very considerable repair | 43 |
| • unfit beyond repair | 28 |

*Hereford Rural District Council*

Conditions were still little better by 1956. Most homes lacked a bath, inside w.c. and piped water. Dr Godfrey Malkin did much to highlight the health risks associated with unsanitary homes. The District Council could have bought four of the 'condemned' houses, including The Folly and Myrtle Cottage on Common Hill, as well as the Court, but declined on the grounds of cost and location.

The census figures for the parish in 1971, taken after the process of improvement was under way, recorded 55 homes without an inside water closet. This number fell to 10 in 1991

|  | No hot water | No bath | No inside w.c. | Lacking one or more |
|---|---|---|---|---|
| 1971 | 54 | 53 | 55 | 62 |
| 1981 | na | 18 | 19 | 19 |

I was at Tanhouse from 1952 to 1970 – I wouldn't have given up but we were constantly getting flooded out from the Tan Brook. You couldn't keep any wallpaper on the walls because of the damp. In July there was a cloudburst during the night, we got up to meet the linoleum coming up and I had to get cleared for nine o'clock. There was mud and silt. *"Right that's it we're going to move"*

*Dora Grant talking to Mandy Dees and Pam Colley 2006*

There was a steady flow of improvement grants from the Council after 1955, rising sharply when mains water and sewerage were installed in the late 1960s, bringing an influx of new owners. Most homes qualified for grants including several which had previously been 'condemned', e.g. Bagpipers, Little Bryalls and The Horns.

Abandoned home            *J Soulsby*   Little Bryalls              *Constable family*

Ossie Edwards asked for a grant in 1955 to upgrade Bark Cottage which was *'grossly neglected'*, damp, had a leaky roof and lacked water and drains. Local opinion, according to the Parish Council, favoured demolition. The District Council gave Ossie a grant of £246 towards the £1079 costs, and reported two years later that the outcome was *'very satisfactory'*. Malthouse, once the village school, was empty and neglected in 1958. Much of the roof was missing, and there was only one cold water tap in the house. The owner, Mrs Dawe, got a grant of £236 towards the £1544 needed to bring the house back to life.

Bark Cottage 2006 *M Clark*    Malthouse 2006 *D M Clark*

More than 90 homes were improved, but grants were refused for some isolated homes without mains water. The Lowe, The Castle, and 11 other homes were abandoned or demolished. These included three cottages on Tump Farm – Whitehall, Lidmore Field and Catchall where George Gwynn lived until 1976. The owners decided to demolish all three – though the new bungalow built next to Tump Farm continued the historic name of Lydmore Field.

Thatching Tump Cottage    *J Soulsby*

The council listed Shears Hill cottage for clearance in 1961 but the occupier Jim Broome, who had been there since the 1940s, remained there without electricity, mains water or road access till his death in 2006.

Shears Hill Cottage    *D V Clarke*    Nash 2005    *D M Clark*

10

# ELECTRICITY

There was no electricity or gas supply in 1919. Heating was provided by coal and wood – with oil and paraffin lamps as recalled here

*Ringfield 1930s* "Keep ourselves warm? – the coal fire in the kitchen was always burning, and the sitting room, which we retired to after meals, but not in the bedrooms"
*Vera E Biggs with Madge Daines & Rachael Best 2005*

*Tump Cottage* "We cooked on oil stoves, oil lamps gave the better light"
*Dorothy Crowe née Pocknell with Pam Colley & Madge Daines 2005*

Melrose's generator powered a circular saw by 1921, and lit the house by 1932, when the *Shropshire, Worcestershire & Staffordshire Company* brought in mains electric to Fiddlers Green and the village. Many homes did not connect, or only used electricity for lighting.

*Tump Farm in the war years* – massive house, so big and cold, it was wartime and coal was restricted, we felled some trees because we were frozen but it was green wood and didn't burn much
*Mabel Williams talking to Pam Colley & Madge Daines 2005*

*Tanhouse 1950s* – We cooked by electricity. We had a big range – you had to heat up – the post office was bitterly cold – in summer I'm still wrapped up in cardigans.
*Dora Grant with Mandy Dees & Pam Colley 2006*

*Tump Farm 1954* – I remember when the electric came to Fownhope. It ended at Mrs. Fox's (Orchard Cottage), we were on top of the hill, we had a generator for electricity for the milking, you had to go to the shed and switch it off at night and come back in the dark and get to bed. We then had the mains electricity brought up the road *about 1954* but it was a very poor supply. Probably ten years later they brought up a PME system and we put three phase electric down to the new barns. I think everybody got it then. When the gas came *(about 1991)* they sent us an application, and we filled it in 'yes' so they had to comply
*Mabel & Michael Williams with Pam Colley & Madge Daines 2006*

The supply was extended to Common Hill in 1953 but it took longer to supply the far end of Capler Lane. The parish council organised a petition for mains gas in 1979 – the supply arrived in the village 12 years later.

# WATER

An abundance of pure water falls from the sky to soak through porous rocks to the clay-line, emerging as springs. Shallow wells have been sunk – operated first by bucket, then by hand pumps from the 18th century. At least 40 wells are marked on maps – some shared between several properties. Some outside wells and brooks could be polluted. Well water was often 'hard' due to the underlying limestone *so* soft rain-water for washing was collected *'off the roof'*.

Coronation pump

Common Hill   *V E Biggs*

A government report in 1935 claimed that Fownhope was relatively well-served compared with the rest of the county:

"Fownhope village supply – The houses in the village up to and including the school and stores have a gravitational supply – owner R.Timbrell, from the Highland Well, a dip-well fed by spring close to the stream and road above Canon House that leads to Common Hill. The pipes were laid many years ago by a Mr. Watkins who had a shop and bake-house in the village. Otherwise the parish is dependent on wells and springs which yield a satisfactory supply."

*Richardson, L, Wells and Springs of Herefordshire, HMSO, 1935*

That did not fit with local opinion. There were frequent complaints about water quality between 1933 and the 1960s. The Jubilee Pump by Tanhouse was closed for a while and water brought by tank from Hereford in 1945. Four public wells were declared unfit in 1949. The Coronation Pump at Common Hill was repaired three times in four years between 1949 and 1953. There were frequent problems at Haughwoodgate. The Nash pump was polluted by surface water in 1954. The spring-fed Island Well was the subject of dispute with the neighbouring farmer at Bowens who had sunk a well which may have reduced the quantity of water at the public well. There was friction between the Parish and Rural District Councils as to who was to blame.

## Fetching Water

*Wyla 1920*   All the drinking water was carried across two orchards to the house.  It was good, beautifully clear water; but I needed an enormous lot on butter making days.

*Helena Biggs (née Watkins), recorded by Margaret Biggs*

*Tump Cottage 1941*   We had our share of fetching a bucket from the pump at the bottom of Woolhope Road.  We had our soft water from the drain pipe for washing clothes.

*Dorothy Crowe talking to Pam Colley 2005*

*Tump Farm 1940s*   A windmill filled the reservoir.  If you had no wind you had no water, it came to a tap in the kitchen, we had a 'ram' down by brook which drew water but in a hot summer the brook dries up so we're out of water, so then the windmill was built.  We'd pump water from the windmill to the reservoir that holds 30,000 gallons, we had a petrol pump to back it up, that was the making of Tump Farm.

*Mabel & Michael Williams talking to Pam Colley & Madge Daines 2005*

*Fern Cottage 1952*   All our water had to be carried from Island Well – we used to save our rain water for washing up.

*Philip Paton, talking to Madge Daines & Pam Colley, 2006*

*Manor Farm 1950s*   The only water supply at that end of the village was from Islands Well, it ran to the Manor, the butchers shop and on to Whiterdine.  We had a well but it didn't work.  We had to carry water in buckets from Islands Well.

*John Westley talking to Mandy Dees and Rachael Best, 2005*

*Nash 1950s*   There was a well opposite the house halfway down the hill and we used to have to go down with buckets and carry it up.  When I was older I used my grandfather's yoke to carry two buckets, you had to knock the toads out of the water.  It probably wasn't the best of water but it didn't do us any harm.

*Derrick Brown talking to Madge Daines & Pam Colley, 2006*

*Fiddlers Green 1952*   We paid £1 a week for *Grove Cottage* and five shillings (25p) for the water, provided from the private supply at Morney Cross.  The Pump House was below the kitchen gardens, and Hans *(the handyman)* would go down three times a week to start the engine to pump water up to a reservoir above Morney Cross.

This reservoir served the household and was fed back down to us by gravitation.

13

We had a pump in the garden but no amount of pumping produced water.  This was the case in many areas.  Dr Malkin, our G.P., and Chairman of the Parish Council, worked long and hard with Mr Foden at the RDC to obtain mains water supply.

*Margaret Biggs 2005*

**Tanhouse 1960**  We got our drinking water from the pump on the corner, two buckets and pump away! We collected soft water off the roof

*Dora Grant talking to Mandy Dees and Pam Colley, 2006*

## Mains Water From Hereford 1937?

Hereford City had enjoyed treated water from as early as 1856 and offered to extend their pipes to rural areas in 1937 but no action could be taken in the war years.  The County Council suggested in 1946 that water could be piped from the city boundary to Mordiford, pumped to a 500,000 gallon reservoir on Backbury Hill, and piped downhill to Fownhope by way of an 8″ main.  There was an alternative plan to pump water from the river at Foy

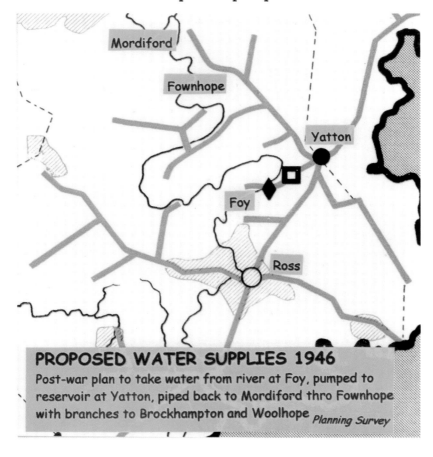

**PROPOSED WATER SUPPLIES 1946**
Post-war plan to take water from river at Foy, pumped to reservoir at Yatton, piped back to Mordiford thro Fownhope with branches to Brockhampton and Woolhope *Planning Survey*

## Borehole Trials

The Parish Council, spurred on by public complaints, pressed the RDC for action. There were more grumpy exchanges and a public inquiry. The RDC dug a series of trial boreholes in Court Orchard, Nupend and Rudge End between 1948 and 1959. They never found more than half the water needed for the village. The Court Orchard borehole could not even meet the needs of the new estate – the water was too hard, and failed the bacteria test in 1954.

## Water Supplies 1955

| private piped supply – inadequate | 45 houses | public well – piped supply | 11 houses |
|---|---|---|---|
| council bore-hole (Court Orchard) | 26 | rest from wells – some shared | 149 |

*from 1955 WI History of Fownhope*

---

**VILLAGE WITH A BIG PROBLEM**

*No more houses until they get a proper water supply*

Biggest problem at Fownhope is, ironically, water. The village that would like so much to expand is in danger of stagnation. Villagers are anxiously awaiting Ministerial permission for a third borehole to be sunk in search of water. Until it is found no more houses can be built in the village, many people will have to continue carrying water up to a quarter of a mile, the school will remain without a water supply.

*Hereford Evening News June 7th 1960*

---

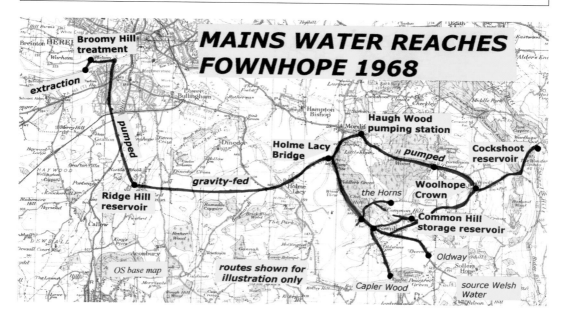

MAINS WATER REACHES FOWNHOPE 1968

### Extracting A Solution 1960-68

Herefordshire Water Board took over from the RDC in 1960. Boreholes plans were scrapped. The Board opted to pipe water from Ross but then switched to a larger scheme to pump from the river Wye above Hereford. The scheme was completed by 1968, just 30 years after it had first been mooted. The scheme included much of Common Hill and Woolhope Road and was extended to include Oldway and Capler Lane, with a second pipe from Holme Lacy Bridge to the village. At long last Fownhope was on mains! Time to install mod cons, and start building. Fownhope would never be the same again!

### and SEWERAGE too!

Two of the big houses, Morney Cross and Rock House, had had inside **water closets** since the early 1870s. They were joined by Whiterdine, Melrose, Bowens and Lea Brink by the 1920s. By the 1950s Morney Cross had three W.C.s and three bathrooms but **five** out of every **six** homes still had no water closet.

**Lechmere Ley 1940s** outside toilets – we had to walk up the garden about 30 yards which wasn't much fun when the weather was iffy

> *Denzil Biggs talking to Madge Daines & Pam Colley, 2006*

**Tump Farm late 1940s** I remember the toilet at the bottom of the garden with two holes, then the huge improvement with the Elsan toilet *'please close the lid when not in use'*, the luxury of the flush came later

> *Jennifer Higham née Williams, talking to Mandy Dees and Pam Colley 2005*

Ferry Lane Pumping Station                    *D M Clark*

## Sewerage Scheme 1969

Plans for mains sewerage in the village, prepared by Major Waters, were shelved as too costly in 1947. A small 'plant' served the new Court Orchard homes in 1952 but the rest of the village had to wait till 1967 for the RDC to approve a £73,454 scheme for drains and sewage works on Malthouse Field, with a pumping station on Ferry Lane. The scheme only served the village despite the efforts of the Parish Council to include Common Hill, Nupend and the west end of Ferry Lane. The contractors, Merjon, delayed by a foot and mouth outbreak, completed the scheme in July 1969. The sewage works were upgraded in 2005 to meet new standards.

Sewage works 2006                                                    *D M Clark*

# DEVELOPMENT

There was virtually no new building in the 33 years between 1919 and 1952 – indeed several homes were abandoned or 'struck down' in the early 1920s including homes on Common Hill, Fiddlers Green and the village.

Times were hard for local builders. Stone Brothers had worked over a very wide area at their peak in the early 1900s. Now competition was stiff, and Reuben Stone had to keep going with house repairs and decorating jobs within a four mile radius of Fownhope. His biggest projects were garages at Mona for the doctor (1922) and Manor Farm (1923), and engine houses for generators at Penrose (1921), Orchard Cottage 1924, and Oldstone Farm (1937)

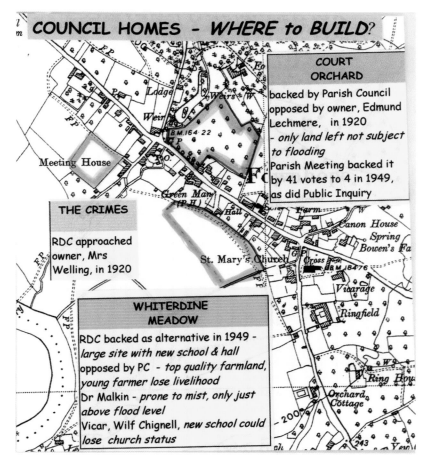

COUNCIL HOMES - WHERE to BUILD?

**COURT ORCHARD**
backed by Parish Council opposed by owner, Edmund Lechmere, in 1920 - only land left not subject to flooding Parish Meeting backed it by 41 votes to 4 in 1949, as did Public Inquiry

**THE CRIMES**
RDC approached owner, Mrs Welling, in 1920

**WHITERDINE MEADOW**
RDC backed as alternative in 1949 - large site with new school & hall opposed by PC - top quality farmland, young farmer lose livelihood Dr Malkin - prone to mist, only just above flood level Vicar, Wilf Chignell, new school could lose church status

## Plans 1951
The first *county Development Plan* listed Fownhope as a *'main' village* in 1951 where new facilities would be linked to extra homes. Fownhope was one of

the few parish councils to actually back the Plan! Mains water and sewerage would be provided along with a new fire station, school and hall, prompting new housing at Court Orchard, Scotch Firs, Fairfield, Church Croft and Nover Wood, more than doubling the size of the village.

## The bid for council housing

The Parish Council had first asked the Rural District Council for four (later, 12) council houses back in 1912. The District Council agreed in 1920 to build on Court Orchard but switched attention elsewhere before returning in 1945 with plans to build 24 homes on Court Orchard. An alternative scheme on Whiterdine meadow met fierce and influential opposition so the RDC reverted to the Court Orchard site which was confirmed by a Public Inquiry in 1949

Court Orchard 2006                    *M Clark*   Reuben Stone      *M Dees*

### Press Reports 1949

*March*    Questions in the House – Nye Bevan, the Housing minister, assured the local MP, J P L Thomas, that he was making every effort, the problem was getting agreement locally

*July*     Newspaper accused RDC and County Council of incompetence, bias and withholding information – Council passed vote of confidence in their Clerk

*Aug*      RDC agreed compulsory purchase for the Court Orchard site – backed by J P L Thomas, local MP

*Nov*      Local councillors, H Fagg and S Pugh, criticised RDC for not giving Fownhope due priority

*Dec*      Lechmere estate objected to the loss of Court Orchard – Public Inquiry required

The scheme was plagued with high costs. The Ministry refused to fund the original £41,800 cost – the RDC had to shave £1,000 off the budget. The Cornish units were shipped in from St Austell, and the contractors travelled in from the Forest of Dean. The land cost £476 an acre, roadworks were costly, and a wall had to be built along the boundary with the Court. Water was a problem – boreholes failed to deliver the required volume, so a Braithwaite tank had to be installed.

The Rural District Council allocated tenancies in 1952 in two stages – 16 of the 38 lived or had lived in Fownhope – three went to key workers (nurse, police, teacher) – the rest to people elsewhere in the district or adjacent areas. Some of those allocated homes – including Joe Chamberlain and John Crowe – decided initially not to move in.

"It's nicer when you've got all mod cons. I can remember them going up. This was all orchard – we used to play in the fields. The farmer was Evan Evans in Manor Farm – a biggish man, always had his thumb stick with him, but he could never chase us because he was too fat!
*Dorothy Crowe talking to Pam Colley & Madge Daines 2005*

Fownhope Parish Council had wanted more development but some residents found it difficult to adjust to newcomers. Wilf Chignell worked to reconcile the old and new:

"It is always a good thing for new blood to come into a village. The days are over when each village was an isolated group who didn't hold with foreigners and those of you who are old inhabitants, should search your hearts to find whether you have welcomed the newcomers as you might. They have new ideas, fresh thoughts and methods. Some may be good. And for those that are new, there is a tendency to think that the old is out of date. But don't think the old village is all bad. It isn't – it was quite healthy before we arrived and will be long after we are gone"
*Church address to the Club Walk 1955* Hereford Times

whilst doing battle with the leaders of the *Tenants Association:*

"Some of those who had come to Court Orchard were much better off than others. The Council decided that the better off ought to pay a higher rent. They formed a Tenants Association. They requested a meeting with Sydney Pugh and myself as councillors ... we had a terrific evening, some of it distinctly unpleasant. I had to bear the brunt. The two leading protagonists shortly afterwards bought houses elsewhere ... nothing more was heard of the Association"
*Wilf Chignell 1948-56 memoirs*

Although most of the first tenants were 'newcomers' many remained and played an active part in village life – eleven of the original families were here 25 years later.

## Local Builders

The Stone Brothers, once a major local employer, closed when the brothers retired in the mid 1960s – just before the building boom!

In their heyday Stone Bros were at the forefront of the local building trades, their vigour seemed to diminish ... they still used the wooden pole system of scaffolding in the fifties

*John Soulsby, The Flag, 1998*

## More Plans

South Herefordshire planners drew limits to future development. The *Conservation Area*, agreed in 1976, required development to be in keeping with the historic character. The *Royal Commission on Historic Monuments* had already earmarked several buildings in 1929 as worthy of protection. Many of these were included in the 'list' published in 1985 of 41 protected buildings, ranging from The Church, Green Man and Nash to the stocks, two mileposts and Tanhouse water pump. The *Settlement Boundary* from 1989, marked the limit to development within the village.

## Scotch Firs

"It was a little black and white house where Dick Brookes lived – he was quite a character ... we used to go into old Mrs Brookes' garden to get lettuce. They had cows. They went from there to *The Folly* at Common Hill"

*Nora Whittall née Samuels talking to Pam Colley & Madge Daines 2005*

Scotch Firs 2006          *Ann Corby*  Church Croft 2006          *D V Clarke*

21

Builders C T Bishop bought Scotch Firs cottage and smallholding (3.6 acres) for £9,750 from Iris Lechmere & her sister Jane Barwell in November 1965. Lechmere's sold the woods *(224 acres)* to a London accountant for £3750. Bishops also bought 2.75 acres from Mervyn Davies of Mill Farm for £2,300 in 1965 – the cash went to re-pay part of a farm mortgage. Bishops completed most of the houses between 1967 and 1969, though No 1, and Scotch Bungalow, were added later. Bishops diverted some footpaths, and imposed covenants restricting occupiers from keeping chickens – unlikely to be enforced as the builder went into liquidation in 1980. Virtually none of the first occupiers came from within the Parish, but many stayed and played an active part in village life.

We weren't on mains before the new Scotch Firs house were built in 1968. Elsie and Harry Smith were the first occupants, and a fortnight later our bungalow was ready, they were building all around us, if you wanted to go out you had to go in the car because your shoes would have been ruined

*Pat Homan talking to Janet Jones & Mandy Dees 2005*

## Church Croft

The prospect of mains water encouraged the RDC to plan more homes adjacent to Court Orchard on Church Croft, as well as a new school, social centre and playing field. Early plans proved too costly, so the RDC decided to increase numbers, and provide communal bathrooms, and toilets for some of the elderly units, which would now be on two floors. Two acres was reserved for a new school. There were differences between county and RDC officers about the status of the playing field, street lighting standards, estate layout, and the junction with Common Hill Lane. The Ministry of Housing disliked the plans for a district heating system. The first planning application was refused – the RDC responded by keeping accommodation separate from the community building. Improvements were made to the junction with Common Hill Lane, and the footpath diverted onto Green Lane.

Work was delayed by a shortage of bricks and adverse weather but was completed in 1972. The village post-mistress, Dora Grant, was appointed as warden of the community centre, renamed as Faulkner House as a tribute to the long-serving chairman of the RDC's Housing committee.

The Bishop of Hereford officially opened Church Croft *(in 1972)*. Now I'm claustrophobic, no way will I use a lift, so My Lord Bishop and myself are standing there, I said *"I'm going up the stairs, I'll meet you".* He said *"I'll hold your hand"*, so I thought *"I've never had my hand held by a Bishop so here goes."*

*Dora Grant talking to Mandy Dees and Pam Colley 2006*

The estate was intended to meet needs from a wide area – however 16 of the first 61 tenants were from Fownhope. Six were still here in 2002, and 7 others have moved within the village. Many of the properties have been bought by tenants and sold onto the open market.

| Nover Wood Drive 2006 | *S Gough* | Nover Wood Drive 2006 | *S Gough* |

## Nover Wood Drive 1974

Church Croft was farmed by the Williams brothers who had bought Manor farm from the Lechmeres for £6,268 in 1960. They in turn sold part of Church Croft to the District Council, and part to builders, T W Pugh, in 1970 for £14,000. Pugh's got planning permission in 1973, diverted footpaths and built roads and sewers. The development took the name of Nover Wood.

The 49 homes were released over a four year period. One typical bungalow, bought in 1974 for £9,100, re-sold in 1982 for £34,500, and again in 1992 for £76,000. Only five of the initial occupiers had lived in the village before but more than a quarter of those first occupants were still in the village 30 years later.

Harry Townsend closed his farm contracting business at Fairfield and sought redevelopment. Plans for 26 homes on the site were turned down in 1975 but 10 homes were built in 1988 as sheltered homes for elderly people.

Fairfield Green          *S Clifford*    Fairfield Green          *S Clifford*

Manor Farm was sold in 1988 to a property developer, Algocin, who renovated the farmhouse, converted the barn and built more homes at the rear. The builder got into financial difficulties and development took three years to complete. Four of the nine buyers remained in the village 12 years later.

Manor Court          *D V Clarke*    Ringfield Drive          *D M Clark*

Many more small scale developments followed. Denzil Biggs retired from his garage business. The planners rejected a scheme for 16 homes on the Ringfield site, but agreement was given in 1993 for six (later seven) homes. Twelve homes were built by Bonds on the east side of Church Croft in 1996. Five homes were built on land alongside the New Inn in 1996, including a house for the landlord, Les Gummery. Five homes were built in 1997 alongside Lower House, served by a new road off the B4224. The Forge and Ferry Pub finally closed, and five homes were built on the pub's car park in 2002.

Church Croft                *D V Clarke*

New Inn Close                *M Clark*

There was infilling within the village envelope too. Richard Biggs at Ringfield sold off two plots to his sons Lionel and Denzil in 1965 for new bungalows. One took the name, Cranstone to commemorate the noted horticulturalist who had lived at Ringfield at the turn of the century. Stoneyhurst was built in part of the garden of Malthouse in 1968.

Deerfield – Lower House Gardens *S Clifford*

Forge Cottages Ferry Lane                *M Clark*

Old Rectory 2006                *D M Clark*

The Folly 2005                *D M Clark*

A new vicarage was built in 1978 on part of the garden of the old vicarage. Part of the garden of Fownhope Cottage was sold off for Hope House, built to a very modern design, albeit within the conservation area. There was infilling on Woolhope Road and the Court drive. Westholme was built next to Scotch Firs in 1993. Netherfield Lodge and Pippins and were built by 1998 on part of Orchard Cottage's garden.

The planners discouraged new homes outside of the village though two new homes were built at Mill Farm and Moorview on Capler Lane. Several barns were converted into homes, including those at Mill, Nupend and Rudge End farms, as well as Swan Barn on Capler Lane. Several isolated properties were gutted and rebuilt often to very different designs.

Beechcroft *S Gough*   Pineview *S Gough*

**Tylers Croft 1975** "We'd spent two or three years, maybe longer, building a bungalow on The Nash. We bought the land off Stanley Hardwick, and built what was at that time the largest bungalow in Herefordshire. We were 22 years at Tylers Croft and moved because it was far too big for us."

*Derrick Brown*

Lidmore Field 2006 *D M Clark*   Little Bryalls *Constable fam*

New homes were created by the conversion of Fownhope Court and the old School into five units, in 1980 and 1994 respectively. Many homes have been substantially altered and extended. Ringhouse had been vacant for many years before it had a serious make-over in 1985. Its neighbour, Ringfield, had been empty for most of the past seven years when Mark Archer spent £60,000 restoring the 'listed' house in 1992.

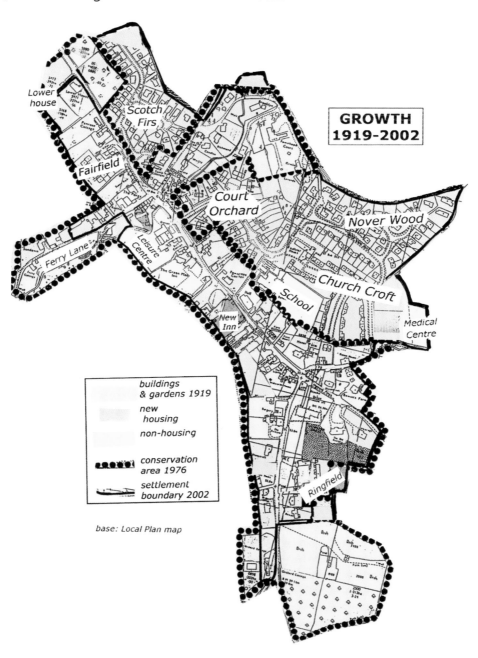

**GROWTH 1919-2002**

buildings & gardens 1919

new housing

non-housing

conservation area 1976

settlement boundary 2002

base: Local Plan map

The development process has transformed the parish over the past 80 years. In 1919 less than 30% of all the homes in the parish (on its modern boundary) were within the village. But since then the number of homes outside the village has actually fallen, whereas the village has grown more than sixfold, so that almost three-quarters of all homes in the parish in 2007 were within the village settlement as defined by the planners. Overall the number of homes in the parish has more than doubled.

|  | *Village* | *Outside the village* | *Total parish* |
| --- | --- | --- | --- |
| 1919 | 51 | 125 | 176 |
| 2007 | 328 | 120 | 448 |
| % change | *Up 543%* | *Lost 4%* | *Extra 155%* |

*adjusted for boundary changes*

Old School                    *Ann Corby*    Hope House                    *D V Clarke*

## Unitary Development Plan 2006

South Herefordshire's plan was replaced by a county-wide plan which took six years to sort out. Fownhope remained a *'main village'* with a line drawn around the village settlement with new building allowed (*as before*) within the envelope. The planners felt that Fownhope had had enough recent building, and that water and sewage facilities were restricted. Nine sites put forward by local landowners were considered but rejected. Four of the sites went to *Public Inquiry* where the Inspector confirmed that no new sites were needed. These four, together with five considered earlier could have accommodated an extra 220 dwellings in the village – an increase of 70% in the size of the village.

Faulkner House                                                                    *M Clark*

Orchard Cottage 2006                                                        *D M Clark*

# FIRE & REFUSE SERVICES

Richard Gange and William Ford acted as fire insurance agents as early as 1868 but the nearest fire engine, in Hereford, must have been of meagre comfort.

*Officers in charge* Harry Fagg 1945-8, Joe Chamberlain 1948-67, Frank Bream 1967-76, John Williams 1976-77, Aeron Davies 1977-94, Tony Limb from 1994

The village fire brigade, aided by the Rural District Council, was in place by 1938 with a manually operated 'pump' stored behind the butcher's shop at Walworth House. It was too late to save the 15th century tithe barn in the vicarage grounds which had burnt down that year. By 1939 the engine was moved to the coach house of Fownhope Court. Two ladies, Ruth and Vera Biggs, had joined the volunteer crew.

*Publican Henry Fagg took over the fire brigade in 1945, moving the 'pump' from Walworth House to Green Man*

David Fry sketch/
Sue Clifford

Harry Fagg, the new publican at the Green Man, took charge in 1945, when the pump moved to his pub, and a siren installed. The crew faced their biggest test in 1948 when three homes in Ferry Lane set on fire.

## FERRY LANE FIRE

Three families were made homeless when a fire gutted three thatched cottages, Nos. 1, 2 and 3 Ferry Row, Fownhope, on Monday afternoon. It is thought the fire may have been started by sparks falling on the roof.

Fanned by a strong wind, the whole roof was ablaze from end to end in a matter of a few minutes, and although the local Fire Unit at Fownhope was on the scene within three minutes, the blaze was already beyond control. Hereford Fire Brigade attended with a water tender and major pump.

One of the occupiers, Mrs R Prince, an elderly widow, had lived in the house for 23 years. An adjoining house was occupied by her son and daughter-in-law, Mr and Mrs G. Prince, and their little boy, aged five months. The third cottage was occupied by Mrs. I. Welling, another widow.

They all lost practically everything they possessed, but a little furniture was salvaged from the downstairs rooms. The cottages were not insured.

Villagers offered shelter for the night. Mr H. G. Fagg, the local representative on the Hereford Rural District Council, got in touch with Mr R.A. Symonds, Clerk to the Council, to see if accommodation could be provided in Fownhope Court, which has been empty for some years. Mr Fagg was also in charge of the local Fire Unit which fought the blaze. He is opening a distress fund to assist the homeless families, and will seek the co-operation of the Parish Council.

*Hereford Times July 1948*

Ferry Lane                                                                 1948 *HRO*

Harry Fagg was succeeded later in 1948 by Joe Chamberlain, gardener to Mabel Fox at Orchard Cottage. Joe had been awarded the BEM for bravery in fighting a fire at the Rotherwas explosive factory in 1945. He served as sub-officer for 19 years. The service was threatened with closure in 1951. The parish meeting mustered some strong objections. Fownhope was the second largest village in the district, had many fire risks, including timbered and thatched homes, large areas of woodland, new development was planned, and the crew had local knowledge. Closure plans were rebuffed again in 1953, and the county opted eight years later to provide a new fire station on Court Orchard, completed in 1963 at a cost of £6,000.

Fire Station 1996                                                                            *Ann Corby*

The new team was called to a major fire at Tump Farm in September 1964. The farmer, Enoch Williams, dialled 999 at 11.23 pm. The crew had just returned from a shout at Pengethley. Joe Chamberlain and the crew of six were at Tump Farm within minutes with support from Hereford and Ross. Even the county fire chief was there within 20 minutes. The water tenders had to shuttle water from the hydrant three quarters of a mile away, and from Tump Farm's own reservoir 500 yards away. Yet again Fownhope's inadequate water supply was exposed. The fire caused £10,000 worth of damage to two Dutch barns. A combine harvester and 300 tons of hay and cereals were lost. The fire was still smouldering next morning, and the crew remained on duty for more than 21 hours. An 18 year old from the village admitted to lighting a match in a moment of temper but was found not guilty of malicious damage.

*Extracts from Joe Chamberlain's report HRO*

I was at home (Rockhurst, Ferry Lane) when the fire bell was activated … firemen were mustered … arrived at Tump Farm at 11.29 pm … two Dutch barns alight … strong wind … red hot sparks. Passageway rendered impassable through heat and smoke ….

The brigade is the only team in the triangle between Hereford, Ledbury and Ross. It serves a wide area and has responded to major fires including Pontrilas in 1970, and Sun Valley in Hereford in 1993. There were 11 'retained' fire fighters in 2005, all of whom live or work within five minutes of the station

Fire Brigade            *Barbara Pritchard*   Tump Farm fire 1964            *HRO*

## Refuse Collection

The Rural District Council introduced the first monthly refuse collection service in 1949 – late even by rural standards. The Parish Council had been asked to organise a voluntary scheme in the war years. Scutterdine Quarry was used as the local tip. Some householders provided their own bins, but most used old boxes. Dustbins were provided for Court Orchard's tenants in 1955. Paper sacks with concrete mountings were introduced in 1967 by which time there was a fortnightly collection. The weekly service was introduced in the 1970s.

Denis Lambert at Stone House collected waste newspaper in 1974 but abandoned it after 9 months because prices were too low. A more ambitious scheme was introduced in September 2004 to collect glass, metal and paper by Ross-based group RE-BOX. They served much of the village, moving from a fortnightly to a weekly schedule in March 2006. The Parish Council arranged a collection facility from 2000 for bulky items in summer months on the Recreation Field. The judges for the *Best Kept Village Competition* were critical of the amount of litter in the village in 1958. The Parish Council responded three years later by providing some litter bins near Court Orchard.

# FARMING

*The principal farmers listed in the 1922 directory were*

| | | | |
|---|---|---|---|
| John Griffiths | *Tump* | Thomas E Robbins | *Rudge End (150a)* |
| John Harper | *Rise* | Capel J Hardwick | *(150a+)/Fruitgr Old Stone* |
| William Ibbotson | *Lower Little Hope* | John Watkins | *Mount Pleasant + Capler Farms* |
| James Pember Biggs | *Ringfield +Manor Farm* | William Mason | *Cottage farmer The Castle* |
| William Thomas | *Mill Farm* | Harry Jauncey | *Upper Little Hope* |

Cows in Ferry Lane            *J Soulsby*

Haymaking            *R Brown*

Most land was under grass though arable land increased in the years up to 1951. Cereals were the main crop – oats and wheat before 1963, barley since then. Pulses and root crops have declined in importance.

The area of orchard declined significantly though the census tends to exclude some small-holdings. Sheep numbers trebled between 1919 and 1988, but cattle peaked in 1974. Several farms turned to pig breeding in the 1960s and 1970s but numbers fell to just one in 1988. Likewise poultry trebled between 1919 and 1951 but has fallen back sharply.

The number of farm units peaked at 52 in 1951 but fell to 16 in 1988. The farm workforce was also declined from 75 in 1941 to 31 in 1988. Stockmen were paid 35s (£1.75) per week in 1929, general farm labourers got 29s (£1.45).

| FARM CENSUS | 1919 | 1929 | 1941 | 1951 | 1963 | 1974 | 1988 |
|---|---|---|---|---|---|---|---|
| land use in acres | | | | | | | |
| Cereals | 348 | 157 | 286 | 292 | 194 | 266 | 294 |
| * Mixed cereal | 8 | 4 | 20 | 43 | 0 | 0 | 0 |
| * Barley | 55 | 32 | 49 | 55 | 76 | 258 | 192 |
| * Oats | 107 | 82 | 127 | 76 | 28 | 0 | 8 |
| * wheat | 178 | 39 | 90 | 118 | 77 | 8 | 94 |
| beans & peas | 84 | 47 | 15 | 19 | 0 | 0 | 27 |
| kale | 0 | 0 | 7 | 15 | 13 | 0 | na |
| root crops | 54 | 51 | 68 | 96 | 100 | 40 | 29 |
| all crops | 508 | 181 | 376 | 422 | 340 | 317 | 360 |
| clover | 80 | 101 | 52 | 126 | 150 | 53 | 112 |
| Permanent grass | 1253 | 1323 | 1189 | 1141 | 1379 | 1501 | 1170 |
| Orchards | 175 | 119 | 195 | 149 | 108 | 70 | 10 |
| arable+pasture+orchard | 1761 | 1582 | 1812 | 1843 | 1978 | 1806 | 1642 |
| rough grazing | 50 | 64 | 40 | 22 | 19 | 65 | 51 |
| livestock numbers | | | | | | | |
| Cattle | 454 | 630 | 614 | 736 | 841 | 1168 | 830 |
| Pigs | 163 | 111 | 109 | 171 | 793 | 2028 | 1 |
| Sheep | 944 | 1336 | 1054 | 1416 | 2628 | 2608 | 2739 |
| Horses | 143 | 63 | 61 | 35 | na | na | na |
| poultry | na | 1665 | 2994 | 4553 | 1733 | 243 | 53 |
| total labour inc family | na | na | 75 | na | na | 46 | 31 |
| farm units | 39 | 42 | 52 | 52 | 48 | 21 | 16 |

*Some variations in information collected*

## The 1941 Farm Survey

Farming was crucial to the country's survival in the war. Government had collected figures from farms since 1866, but the surveys were widened in 1941 to provide a complete picture of each farm and small-holding, even an independent inspector's rating of each farmer – something which must have been far from popular.

Most of Fownhope was down to grass. Almost every holding over 20 acres had some cereals. There was relatively little land under root crops – 67 acres – and this was mainly on the larger farms. Almost every holding had some orchards. Bowens however was the only farm where the majority of land was in orchards – though many cottage gardens were predominantly orchard. Some larger farms, such as Tump (8%) and The Rise (3%) had relatively little orchard land.

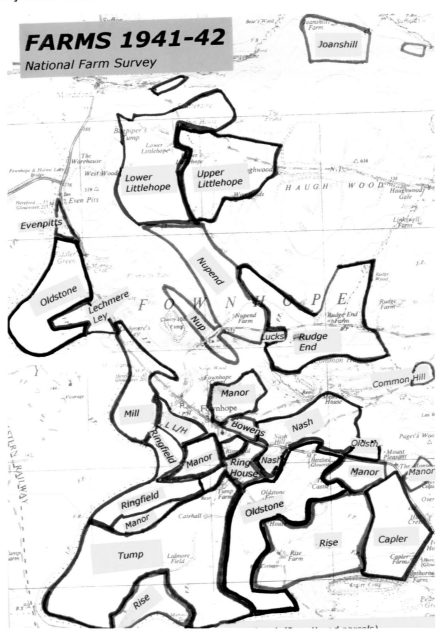

Most farms had some milch cows but none could be called a dairy farm. Beef numbers were high on Nupend, Rise and Tump, while Tump, Rise, Capler, Manor, Ringfield, and the Littlehopes had a large number of sheep. Fowls were particularly important on the smallholdings. Ringfield had a flock of 116 ducks. Most of the larger farms kept horses but few kept pigs.

## FARMS                                    1941 SURVEY

| Holding | farmer | acres | ft? | Class |
|---|---|---|---|---|
| Bagpipers Tump | J Alford | 5 | hf | B |
| Bowens | H Matthews* | 27 | ft | A |
| Caplor | M Williams | 82.5 | ft | A |
| Common Hill Farm | W Robinson | 20 | st | A |
| Common Hill House | Ms Marshall* | 8 | hf | A |
| Eastwood | Mrs Berry* | 14 | ft | A |
| Evenpitt | A Morgan* | 15 | ft | A |
| Fishpool Hill | Mrs Scaffold | 14.5 | ft | C |
| Joans Hill | A Warren* | 48 | ft | A |
| Lechmere Ley | R E Biggs | 29.5 | ft | A |
| Lower Littlehope | Greenow | 100 | ft | C |
| Lower Fishpool Hill | Handford* | 8.5 | st | A |
| Lucksall | A Powell* | 21.5 | ft | A |
| Manor Farm | E Evans | 88.5 | ft | A |
| Mill Farm | Cloke | 88 | ft | X |
| Moon Inn | Holbrook | 5.5 | st | A |
| Mordiford Mill | Mrs G Webb | 5 | hf | A |
| Morney Cross | Maj Dane* | 14 | hf | A |
| Mount Pleasant | Mrs Watkins | 16 | ft | A |
| Nash | J M Sayce | 78 | ft | C |
| Nupend | Mrs S Howells | 138 | ft | A |
| Oldstone | Mrs Hardwick | 223 | ft | A |
| Ringfield | W J Dawe | 60 | ft | B |
| Ringhouse | Hg Jauncey | 13.5 | ft | A |
| Rudge End | Robbins* | 100 | ft | C |
| Rudge End | Rickatts | 15 | pt | A |
| Rudge End Cottage | Cooke* | 8 | pt | A |
| Springfield | Godsell | 7 | pt | A |
| Tan House | R J Stone* | 20.5 | st | B |
| The Rise | Mrs Stone | 141 | ft | A |
| Tump | Williams | 258 | ft | A |
| Upper Littlehope | E Jancey | 81 | ft | B |
| Yew Tree | A Stone* | 17.5 | st | B |

*= owner occupiers; inspectors rated for ability & effort
– A excellent   B adequate   C poor   X new tenant
st/hf = spare time & halftime, often with other work

Government encouraged farmers to plough up land to help make the country self-sufficient. Local farmers had ploughed up almost a fifth of the pasture land (157 acres) by 1941, planting a mixture of oats (85 acres), wheat (9.5), mixed cereal (28), and a small amount of potatoes and beans.

### SMALLHOLDINGS 1941

|  | occupier | Acres | type |
|---|---|---|---|
| Ash Cottage, Common Hill | W Pocknell |  | poultry |
| Common Hill | Rowberry. J | 4 |  |
| Ferry Lane | Welling | 1 | poultry |
| Glenridge | A E Oakley | 4 | cottage |
| Grove, The | Grundy, Mrs E | 2 | poultry |
| Hazlewood | T A Jones |  |  |
| Lower House | Shelton, Ch | 2 | cottage |
| Mangerdine | Green, B E | 3 | poultry |
| Moon Inn | Holbrook |  |  |
| Mordiford Mill | Mrs G Webb | 5 | cottage |
| Myrtle Cottage, Common Hill | F Harrison | 3 | poultry |
| Nash Villa | Thos Stone | 3 | poultry |
| Orange Tree, Common Hill | Sutherland, A | 4 | orchard |
| Rise Cottage | Biggs, Miss A |  | poultry |
| Scotch Firs Cottage | Brookes, Jas | 3 | cottage |
| Stone House, Common Hill | Ferry, Geo | 3 |  |
| Stubblecroft Ct, Common Hill | Pocknall, John |  | poultry |
| The Castle | Andrews, D | 4 | cottage |
| Whitegate | Leslie-Tompson | 4 | cottage |
| Wylow | Mrs A E Taylor | 4 | orchard |
| Yew Tree Cott, Common Hill | C Clarke | 2 | cottage |

**Oldstone**, one of the larger farms, has been farmed by six generations of Hardwicks including Capel and Edith, Stanley and now John and Geoffrey.

It was a mixed farm, milking cows, grandmother made butter, poultry, traditional Hereford cattle, breeding ewes, pigs, arable, cider fruit. Grandfather studied horticulture in Edinburgh, came back and planted an orchard of Bramley and Newton apples.

In my childhood (1950s) we used to help at weekends cleaning pigs out, feeding the poultry, dagging lambs, and picking fat lambs to kill in Monday's market. We used to run close to 100 sows here – if the store trade wasn't brilliant, we used to fatten them, so we had 500-600 pigs on the farm … primarily large White cross Landrace, or Welsh cross Saddlebacks. In 1986 we sold £20,000 worth of pigs, it cost us £20,000 to feed them, so we decided to get out of pigs.

In 1995 we doubled the beef cattle numbers – and moved out of sheep. It suited the farm and the labour situation at the time. We were due to export beef to Italy at £2.60 a kilo in 1995 but after the BSE *(mad cow disease)* announcement there was no market for beef, even now the price is only £1.95 a kilo.

Father lost all the stock on the farm in the foot and mouth outbreak in the 1940s – it upset him a good deal. This time (2001) we were not allowed to move or sell stock, or clean the sheds out and take the muck across the road. We went nearly 12 months with no income coming in. Animal welfare rules went out of the window. The ones that got Foot and Mouth were better off than the ones that didn't.

*John Hardwick of Oldstone talking to Pam Colley & Rachael Best 2006*

Oldstone from air 1965                    *Sky*

Oldstone buildings 2006          *D M Clark*

**Lechmere Ley** was owned by the Hardwicks and let to Richard Biggs from the 1930s to the 1950s

Cider was made in November/December. Apples taken by pony and float to Mill Farm or Tan House. The pony pushed the mill wheel to crush the fruit. A bacon pig was raised … mother would prepare hams, sides of bacon, black pudding and faggots, even the bladder was "blown" and used as a football.

We had a small dairy herd of six to eight cows, we supplied 'free milk' to the School. Cows were milked by hand until a Gascoigne machine was bought after the War. The surplus went to butter and skim fed to the animals.

During winter cows were kept inside. They had to be fed, watered and cleaned out twice a day – a lot of water was needed.

Hay making was a busy time. The grass was cut by a machine pulled by two cart horses, turned into a *"tedder"*, then put into rows, then into *"cocks"*, piles of hay ten yards apart. Jim Brookes from Scotch Firs brought his carthorse with a wagon, we loaded by hand and made into ricks, and stored in a new Dutch barn at Lechmere Ley.

*Lionel Biggs 2006*

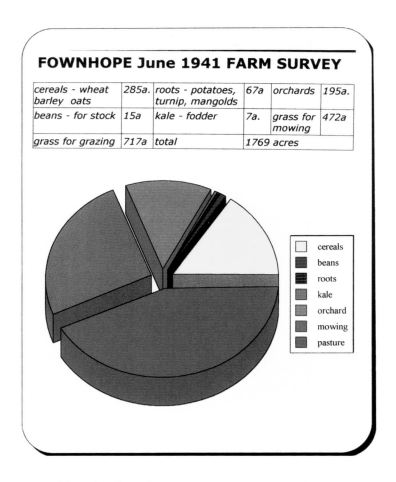

**FOWNHOPE June 1941 FARM SURVEY**

| cereals - wheat barley oats | 285a. | roots - potatoes, turnip, mangolds | 67a | orchards | 195a. |
|---|---|---|---|---|---|
| beans - for stock | 15a | kale - fodder | 7a. | grass for mowing | 472a |
| grass for grazing | 717a | total | | 1769 acres | |

cereals
beans
roots
kale
orchard
mowing
pasture

**Rise** Farm, owned by the Brockhampton estate, was farmed by the Harpers till 1933, then by Ada and later by Archie Stone till the 1990s. **Tump** Farm, the largest holding in the parish, was farmed by John Griffiths till he retired in 1928, when Enoch Williams took over, to be followed by Michael and now Martin who farms 400 acres.

We'd plough as many as five times to get the depth for potatoes whereas now you go with a rotary cultivator with a drill on top, once over. It was organic farming in those days – not much fertiliser, no sprays, lots of poppies, a few thistles. The binder cut the corn into sheaves, then you'd put six to eight sheaves in a stook, leave them out for three Sundays, otherwise they'd go mouldy in the ricks.

It used to be crawling with rabbits prior to the combine harvester. Dad used to be able to catch a rabbit in the rows of straw. When the floods came the rabbits got up the trees, and he'd go and catch them but I've never done too much rabbiting.

*Michael Williams Tump Farm talking to Madge Daines & Pam Colley 2006*

Lechmere Ley          *S Clifford*          Rise Farm 2006          *D M Clark*

(Tump) Very much a mixed farm in the 1950s, 300 acres, dairy, lot of sheep, not a lot of poultry, lot of arable. I remember harvesting and sorting potatoes, and the apple harvest, putting them in sacks to send to Bulmers, and the wonderful working horses called Bonnie and Diamond. We used to deliver milk in Fownhope with pony and trap, with Rhoda Owens who lived in one of the farm cottages. There were no fridges then so a daily delivery. We had churns, buckets and metal ladles. We progressed to milk bottles with cardboard tops, then to foil.

*Jennifer Higham, née Williams, with Mandy Dees & Pam Colley 2005*

Tump Farm from air 1965          *Sky*          New barns below Catchall 2005  *D M Clark*

Barn above Lea Brink          *D M Clark*          Cereals near Mansells Ferry          *D M Clark*

**Capler**, an 80 acre farm, was up for sale in 1921. Morgan Williams took on the farm when the Greenow's moved on to Mill Farm in 1925. It has been farmed by three generations, Morgan, David and Gareth.

Capler Farm house 1934     *Alf Watkins*   Ringfield from air     *Sky*

**Ringfield**, home of the Apperleys, had been the largest farm (380 acres) in the parish in the 1870s, but much of the land had been let off by the 1920s. It was farmed by James Pember Biggs, then by William Dawe who retired in 1957, when the farm was sold to Richard E Biggs from Lechmere Ley.

Ringfield orchard 2006     *D M Clark*   Manor Farm  L Haines with horse  *J Soulsby*

The orchard next to us belonged to Dick Biggs of Ringfield. We used to feel guilty because they always picked the apples and put them in sacks underneath the trees very meticulously and regularly at the right times.
*Jill Howard Jones talking to Pam Colley & Mandy Dees 2006*

**Bowens**, a 27 acre farm, was occupied by the Matthews family from 1905 to 1979 when the house became a guesthouse. Evan Evans farmed **Manor** Farm's 88 acres from 1919 to 1957 when Derrick Williams took over. Much of the farm was later sold for development.

Manor Farm 1987      *Jane Davies*    Manor Farm 1987      *Jane Davies*

**Mill Farm's** 90 acres was put up for sale by the Lechmeres in 1921. It was farmed by Greenow and Price and by Clem Hall before Mervyn Davies took over in 1946, staying 40 years.

Mill Farm 1913      *Ann Morris*    Mill Farm 1950s      *Anne Morris*

I joined the Land Army in 1920, came to Ross from Kent, met my husband Merv who farmed at Brampton Abbots and moved to Mill Farm in 1945. There was no electric. We had an oil cooker. We got water from a well at the back door which had to be pumped to a tank to feed the kitchen tap. Mill Farm was dairy – milk and calves, a few pigs, with potatoes, sugar beet and grass for feed. We had some help, particularly at potato harvests. Our milk was collected by the Milk Marketing Board.

*Joan Davies talking to Madge Daines & Pam Colley 2005*

I left Fownhope school at 15 and went to work at Mill Farm as cowman to Merv Davies. I milked 25-40 cows by machine, milked three at once. I started milking at 5.30am to be ready for collection at 8am. The Ayrshire herd won prizes in shows. I enjoyed the work but the money wasn't good. I earned four times as much when I left to work in building.

*Bill Taylor talking to Pam Colley & Madge Daines 2007*

Rudge End Farm 1950s     *S Clifford*     Robbins at Rudge End Farm 1950s  *S Clifford*

The Robbins family farmed 180 acres at **Rudge End** from 1917 to 1968 when Alan and Kath Watkins took over.

"A mixed farm – store cattle were reared up from calves for market – my people weren't interested in fattening animals.

We used to milk about three or four cows, more or less just for ourselves. A few people used to come and buy it by the quart in those days at the door. Mum made butter.  In the winter time when things were bad you didn't get a lot but in the summer you had a surplus of milk which you could make into cream – you would take the cream off the top.  We had a separator you poured the milk into, turned the handle and a big whirling thing would go round and throw cream outside.  She used to make butter always on a Monday; that was her washing and butter day."

*Harry Robbins talking to Janet & Ian Jones 2006*

Arthur Powell farmed 21 acres at **Lucksall** in conjunction with his timber and coal business.

In the 1930s I milked the cows.  We delivered by pony and trap.  We had an urn and bucket and measured pints and half pints into jugs.  We sold butter in half-pounds.  We delivered to Fownhope, Holme Lacy and Mordiford.  We polished the urn and bucket every day and scrubbed the trap out.

*Mabel Williams née Powell talking to Madge Daines & Pam Colley 2005*

**Lower Littlehope**, a 100 acre farm, became a major pig business in the 1950s.

Father, H R Griffiths, bought Lower Littlehope in 1953 for £7,300 – renamed it 'Hope Springs'.  We restored the rundown buildings and put in 300-400 bacon pigs, relying on swill feed from schools and cafés in Hereford and Monmouthshire.  Couldn't get lean enough bacon, so we switched to pork, sold to the *Fatstock Marketing Corporation*, or to market in Gloucester.  We got out of pigs by 1985. We grew wheat, barley and oats, and built up a dairy herd of Friesians. It was a closed herd with our own resident bull. Milk was collected daily at the Moon Inn for Cadburys at Leominster. We had a Ferguson tractor. Harry Townsend at Fairfield brought his combine harvester, thresher and baler.

*Derek Griffiths with Pam Colley & Madge Daines 2007*

Hope Springs Farm                    *P Daines*

Tyler family hops                    *D Brown*

Four of our neighbour's pigs got into our back kitchen at Wylow and managed to eat the long bars of soap we kept there. We chased them back to their fold. Next day we asked him how his pigs were. *"Pigs? Had to put them down. Frothing at the mouth, probably got swine fever so we shot 'em and buried 'em!"*

*Noel Taylor of Citterdine with Madge Daines & Pam Colley 2006*

Joanshill Farm                    *Liv Moss*

Joanshill Farm                    *Liv Moss*

**Joans Hill** a remote 50 acre farm, was owned by Sam Warren for 42 years from 1937. His early accounts give a good idea of how farmers had to make everything pay. At least half his income of £236 a year (equal to £8300 in 2005) came in the monthly milk cheque from Cadburys, augmented by seasonal sales of cider fruit, mistletoe, mushrooms, blackberries. He sold beasts two or three times a year and took sheep cattle and rabbit skins to

45

Hereford market. He managed to run a motor bike or car on his meagre income. His daughter Liv Moss recalls:

"Dad originally had sheep but they kept getting out. We never had hops although the kilns were functional. He used Harry Townsend (the contractor at Fairfield) for threshing. Father sowed seeds with a fiddle, and used a Welsh mare to draw the plough and horse rake.

When ploughing, our old sheepdog would follow up and down all day. The hay was stooked and put up loose on the cart with Mum on top to weight it down!

I had great fun playing in the hay meadows, jumping on the stooks, and climbing on the rick. Dad used to cut bean and pea sticks for 5s a bunch, sell rabbits and pigeons, and delivered milk in Checkley to earn a crust!

We used to have such a lot of wild flowers, bee orchids, oxlips, wild columbines, kingcups, cowslips, trefoils, centaury, ragged robin, common orchids, wild scabious, pink blue and white violets. We heard the nightingale often, and saw hares boxing in the fields."

Fred Leyman built up a substantial market garden at **Stone House** from 1934.

He came to Stone House from Woolhope, taking over from Averay Jones. He started a nursery – grew flowers, plants, trees, vegetables, and tomatoes, made bouquets and wreaths. Father had stalls in the Butter and Cattle Markets, and people called at the nursery. Stone House had electricity and running water, with extra water from a pumped bore hole. My father, Matthew Leyman, closed the nursery in 1971 and moved to Dormington.

*Pip Leyman with Mandy Dees & Pam Colley 2005*

Mr Leyman at Hereford Market

Stone House glasshouse          *Pip Leyman*

I worked in Leymans garden from 4 till 7 pm every day from the age of 11. Leymans grew plants, cut flowers, and geraniums. I helped with the bouquets and wreaths, and did deliveries on bike to the nuns at Court and to Holme Lacy station. I earned 7s 6d a week.

*Rose Pullen née Godsell talking to Rachael Best & Pam Colley*

Pennybrook from air          *Sky*    The Grove 2006          *D M Clark*

## Smallholdings

Many families combined cottage farming with other work.

We lived at one of the Capler Wood cottages, rented by Archie Stone at Rise Farm from the Clays. We had to carry water from near Irongates. My husband cycled to work. We kept pigs, poultry, turkeys and ducks.

*Phyllis Yarranton née Alford talking to Mandy Dees and Pam Colley 2006*

Scotch Firs                                        *David Fry / S Clifford*

A small vineyard was set up at Halfpenny House *(now Clearview)* on Common Hill Lane in the late 1980s. Lavinia and Giles Cross had their grapes processed by the *Three Choirs winery* near Newent – for home consumption!

47

Cider mill, Mill Farm    *P Daines*    Cider apple harvest, J Whistance                    *S Gough*

## Contractors

Harry Townsend was in business as a threshing contractor in Brockhampton in the 1920s, moved to Ringfield by 1933, and on to Fairfield by 1939 where he stayed to the early 1970s. He was one of the first to have a combine harvester.

Fairfield from air 1965              *Sky*    Harry Townsend                    *S Clifford*

# WORK IN THE WOODS

Haugh Wood extends into Woolhope and Mordiford parishes. Over half of the woodland was managed in 1919 as *'coppice'* – cut after 18 to 20 years for poles, fencing and for bark, particularly from oak wood. The woods were divided into sections or lots – with at least one section ready to cut each year. Felling rights to the 'fallage' were sold at auction at *the Green Man, the Crown* at Woolhope, or *the Moon* at Mordiford.

Williams and Tylers workers                                                                 *D Brown*

The bulk of the wood, owned by the Lord of the Manor, Mrs Wood Acton, was sold to the state-owned *Forestry Commission* in 1925. The Commission replaced deciduous trees with conifers, particular larch, which grew more quickly, though some beech was also planted. They had to contend with natural re-growth of old coppice timbers and needed more wood-men. The Sufton estate continued coppicing until the Commission acquired their part of the woods in the 1950s.

"Dad worked in the woods in the 1940s to control the pests. He set snares, trapped rabbits, and shot grey squirrels. I helped him in the school holidays. He got 10d (4p) for every squirrel's tail. We ate the rabbits. He would go out at 7.30 am, and was back at 5 pm. He took cold tea, bread and cheese with him. He would walk out as far as Joans Hill."

*Bill Taylor talking to Pam Colley & Madge Daines 2007*

Bill Evans worked in Haugh Wood as a teenager during the war. He recalled that the woods were somewhat neglected due to a shortage of labour, though some Latvian and Polish refugees were billeted to work in the woods, as well as some 20 girls from the land army who cut pit props with bush saws. Some 20 or so German prisoners of war made willow baskets. Work could continue till midnight in summer. Some relics of coppicing were revived. Bark was cut from 200 oak trees in 1950 by Albert 'Cutter' Davies, who lived at Haughwood Cottage, using the old tools. Some hazel bundles were sold. A RAF plane crashed in the woods near Rudge End quarry in 1944 killing the pilot.

Haugh Wood 2006                                                               *D M Clark*

Bill's brother Dennis worked in Haugh Wood for many years –
"Most of the team came from Woolhope and Fownhope but numbers were reduced to just five by 1990 because the *Forestry Commission* sold the felling rights to outside contractors. We didn't work beyond 3.30 pm in winter because it got too gloomy amongst the Douglas firs. We didn't like being idle on wet days – we spent the time in the old Nissen hut cutting wood.
Saplings came from the Forest of Dean, North Wales and the Netherlands. We could plant 500 saplings by hand in one day when the conditions were right. Larch took 65-70 years to mature, ash 80 years, oak 150 years.
Horses, kept at local farms, were used to thin the rows but were replaced by machinery later. New 'roads' were built through the woods with material from the Ross Railway when it closed in the 1960s. These new roads brought

in many more walkers. Timber was sold as pit props to the Forest of Dean, for fencing, and the bark had been shipped from Holme Lacy station.

We had to net the young trees. George Taylor from Nupend was employed as trapper to deal with the grey squirrels and rabbits – though rabbits were reduced by *myxomatosis*.

We didn't have much trouble with deer, though they were a nuisance to neighbouring farmers. The Commission sold shooting rights, but didn't publicise that too much because the public didn't like the idea."

*Dennis Evans talking to Pam Colley & Madge Daines 2007*

West Wood                    *D M Clark*  Nupend                *D M Clark*

The *Forestry Commission* decided that English conifers could not compete with Swedish and Canadian firs. They opted to give greater priority to wildlife in the mid 1980s, planting more than two acres of ash and cherry in 1991. Haugh's conifers and larches are being replaced by native deciduous trees such as oak, ash and beech, by natural regeneration and some re-planting. The Commission decided to revert to coppicing, and will have a range of coppice products available by 2020. All uncut timber is now sold at auction to contractors – *Forestry Enterprise* does no felling itself.

# SERVICES & SHOPS

Fownhope in 1922 offered a range of places to shop and drink.  You could even pay your taxes and rates in the village

| Frederick Jones | Tax & Rates Collector | Alpha Cottage |
|---|---|---|
| Jane Wellings | Beer Retailer | Highland Home |
| Fred Goode | Carrier/ Beer Retailer | New Inn |
| Reuben & James Stone | Builders | Tan House |
| George Biggs | Coal Merchant | 1 West Villas |
| Mary Dyer | Dressmaker | Bark Cottage |
| Harold I Monkley | Grocer | Manchester House |
| Roland Timbrell | Grocer / Tea Dealer | The Stores |
| Esther Samuel | Innkeeper | Green Man PH |
| William Shock | Innkeeper | Anchor PH |
| Hettie Brown | Postmistress/Stationer | Post Office |
| John Pritchard | Butchers | Walworth House |
| Thomas Newman | Miller | Mordiford Mill |
| Arthur Powell | Timber Dealer/Gates/Coal | Lucksall |

*Kellys Directory 1922*

Walworth House 1907

*V E Biggs*

The dressmaker, miller and tax collector had gone by 1939, but other businesses survived despite the falling population and improved transport links to Hereford. One new shop opened – the grocer/newsagent at West End Stores. Fownhope gained two garages by the 1950s, as well as an ironmonger and hairdressing salon in the early 1970s when the village grew in size. On the down side Stones ceased in the mid 1960s, followed by the Anchor Inn (*road widening*) in 1972, The Stores about 1975, the ironmonger in 1988, Biggs garage in 1993, and finally the Forge and Ferry pub in 2001. It would be easy but inaccurate to portray this as an inevitable decline in rural services. New businesses have more than made up the losses – notably the Medical Centre, Bowens guesthouse, the Leisure Centre and River Bed restaurant.

## *Walworth House*

Walworth House had been a shop since the 1850s, occupied by butchers from the 1860s. John Pritchard took over from Harry Betteridge in 1919, combining with his business in St Owens Street in Hereford where he lived.

---

**BUTCHER'S SHOP**

Slaughterhouse, fasting pen, boiler house, motor house, traphouse, sheds and yard, in the occupation of Messrs Pritchards and Sons.

Successful butcher's business has been carried on for many years.

Cottages adjoining occupied by Wilfred Grundy and Walter Smith.

*Hereford Journal Sept 1929*

---

Walworth 2006          *Ann Corby*

Walworth 2006          *Ann Corby*

John and his sister Nora Pritchard bought the shop from the landlords in 1929. John and Joyce lived in the adjoining house from 1936 to 1963.

"Julia Pocknell who went to our excellent butcher's shop would never accept the first piece of meat Mr Pritchard would offer her, always chose something else. Mr Pritchard said her choice was often inferior."

*Chignell memoirs 1956*

53

"Pritchard's butchers used to do their own slaughtering of sheep and cattle in the slaughter house in the 1950s, still there behind the shop. I don't recall any noise. Most old families kept their own pigs and chickens and had a pigs cot in the garden. Jack Pritchard used to go round slaughtering in back gardens."

*P Paton, talking to Madge Daines & Pam Colley 2006*

In the 1970s Joyce Prichard used to sit at the till in fingerless woollen gloves during the cold weather – absolutely numb with cold. There was no heating in the shop, she'd sit there under an un-shaded light bulb, just before Christmas till two in the morning

*Jill Howard Jones talking to Pam Colley & Mandy Dees 2006*

Philip Pritchard joined his mother Joyce about 1965, and continued to the 1990s. He lived at Richmond in Fownhope Grove. He offered meat *"direct from the farm, top grade bacon, all poultry, deep freezes catered for at competitive prices and a daily delivery service" (Parish Magazine 1974)*

The butcher was fabulous as everybody will tell you. People come from far away to use him. I used to say Philip Pritchard worked longer hours than Patrick. Yes a very hardworking man.

*Mary Ramage talking to Pam Colley & Margaret Clark, 2006*

Brian and Ruth Stanton took over the shop in 1996 and continued trading as J A Pritchard. They source their meat locally and deliver within a 10 mile radius of the village.

The Stores                                                                    *B Snape*

54

## The Stores

The Stores had been the main grocer from the 1850s, long associated with John Watkins and his family. Roland Timbrell from the Cotswolds had taken over as grocer, tea dealer, baker and corn merchant in 1912. He stayed for twenty years till he retired in 1933 when Lloyd and Mildred James took over.

Tea van by The Stores 1930s?    *J Soulsby*    The Stores from air 1965    *Sky*

---

Excellent Country Business Premises General Grocer and Confectioner
**THE STORES, FOWNHOPE**
Commodious premises; Double-fronted Shop, Storerooms, Bakery;
large Lounge, Living Room at rear of shop, first floor 4 Bedrooms & Bathroom
Useful Warehouse and Store-room Subject to tenancy rental £60 per annum
Frequent bus service passes the door. Telephone installed. Main electricity

*Hereford Times June 1951*

---

The Stores sold for £1,925 in 1951. The James remained as tenants till 1953 when Geoff and Jocyln Thomas kept the stores, followed by Gerald and Elizabeth Baylis from 1960 to 1970

"General stores called 'Baylis' was up the steps opposite the school. We'd buy ham and bread and basic stuff from there."
*Mary Ramage talking to Pam Colley & Margaret Clark 2006*

The Stores was empty before Robert and Jenny Harris-Mayes tried to revive trade but opted to close the shop about 1975 when it became a private house, renamed as Cassiobury.

## Manchester House

Manchester House had been a shop since the 1850s – once a draper's shop as the name implies. William and Sarah Clarke kept it as a grocer's shop and bakery from 1917 to 1920 when Harold I Monkley took over *as 'family grocer, corn, flour and cake merchant'*. Monkley also owned the wheelwright's cottage behind the shop. Monkley gave way to Edward A Hancorn in 1930 who stayed for 24 years till Wilf Grundy came in 1954. Sam and Annie Bould succeeded in 1959, but lived next door in Alpha Cottage. Ted and Olive Pocknell took over in 1961.

Manchester House 1913                                                    *Ann Corby*

"When we bought the shop it was awful, no more than a lock-up, with one electric light and no water. The three young women employees had to go next door to Alpha House to use the toilets. We decided not to continue any bakery work, and bricked up the oven. We ran a delivery business with the estate car, with weekly rounds to Ross, Holme Lacy, Woolhope and Brockhampton. Around 1970 we took over the post office contract from Mrs Grant. We sold the shop in 1976 to Mr Ball."

*Ted Pocknell talking to John Gill & David V Clarke, 2006*

"Pocknells was a well-stocked friendly village shop and post office. Mr and Mrs Pocknell were very accommodating, would deliver even a small order ... just a couple of toilet rolls and he'd be round. I can see Mr Pocknell now, a little white haired man, quite plump, in his white overall, looking up the price of Marmite in his little book, I'd wait for ages while he'd check the price ... he deserved every penny."

*Jill Howard Jones*

The Pocknells stayed next door at Alpha Cottage when they sold the business in 1976 to Anthony and Ann Ball. The inventory at their sale in 1993 gives some idea of the business – bacon slicer, Lyons Maid ice cream freezer, and cheese cutting board. Four of the five part-time staff lived in Fownhope, were paid £3 an hour, with 2 weeks annual holiday. Anthony and Ann Corby ran the shop for three years between 1993 and 1996. Their successors Robert and Angie Thompson stayed just 9 months. The post office work moved to West End Stores. The shop was empty for 18 months until Austyn and Sue Clifford converted it to antiques, adding gifts, gallery, tea room in 2003. The shop was renamed Marjorie's Moon in 2006.

Manchester House 1950s          *S Clifford*     The Gallery                      *S Clifford*

## West End Stores

The store has had four owners in 80 years. Thomas and Edith Collings started a grocery shop in 1925. Harry and Ada Lloyd took over in 1927. The shop was called a newsagents in 1937, though they also sold ice-cream and tinned goods. The Lloyds lived next door in Willow Cottage.

West End stores 1930s          *B Snape*     West End stores 1960s            *S Clifford*

Harry, chairman of the Parish Council in the war years, put the business up for sale in 1945.

---

*By order of the owner who is leaving, West End Stores, Fownhope*

The whole of the attractive household furniture and effects, viz., 2 oak pan bedsteads, spring and wool mattresses, 2 small modern oak bedroom suites, carpets, chests of drawers, singer treadle and hand sewing machines, all mains electric wireless set, walnut writing desk, Brilliant toned iron frame cottage pianoforte by Bord, electric cooker, kettle and iron, kitchen cabinet, culinary utensils, china and glass, also the outdoor effects: portable sweet stall, ice cream maker and stand and storage cabinet, gents Raleigh cycle and Hercules cycle with box side car, galvanised iron corn bin, buckets, dust bins and water tank, extension and other ladders, three pairs steps, rolls wire netting and chain link fencing, galvanised iron sheets, pig troughs, wheelbarrow, marquee 30 ft × 16 ft in good condition, quantity paints, 2 cwt wire nails, half cwt red oxide, 75ft rubber hose, platform scales, hand operated petrol pump, garden roller, etc., 15 strong store pigs, 20 head poultry, 5 ducks etc., on view morning of sale.  No catalogues

*Hereford Times 21 April 1945*

---

Herbert and Mary Lawler took over and lived over the shop.  Harry is remembered as a Quaker and Labour party supporter.  He also sold fireworks before bonfire night.

"A little shop in those days (1950s), a lot smaller than it is now, a door at the front and a little shed off to the left which was open in summer to sell ice cream – that was a real treat.  On Sundays it was only open for papers because that was all they were allowed to sell in those days."

*Derrick Brown talking to Pam Colley & Madge Daines 2006*

Bernard & Marjorie Wargen 1990  *S Clifford*    West End 2005                    *D M Clark*

Bernard and Irene Wargen took over in 1970 with help from family members including daughter Sue –

"The shop and house were cold in the 1970s with no comforts. You had to go through a huge barn to get to the kitchen and bathroom. We sold paraffin, petrol, oil as well as newspapers and tobacco. We were open for two hours on Sundays to sell papers, with a hut outside which did a good trade in ice creams. Trade expanded in the mid 1970s to include groceries including local produce such as fruit from Margaret Mais at Nupend Mill and cakes from Margaret Williams at Caplor. The off-licence came in the 1980s and has done well. Petrol sales stopped when the Garage was open about 1992. The Post Office switched here from Manchester House in 1997. There wasn't enough business for two shops."

*Sue Clifford née Wargen with Madge Daines & Pam Colley 2007*

Roy Wargen did the paper round.

"The papers were collected from town at 5.30am. My brother Royston did most of the round. Numbers grew to around 300 homes in Fownhope, Mordiford, Sufton, and Woolhope, extended later to How Caple, Hampton Bishop, Kings Caple and even Hoarwithy. It took 4hours to deliver Hoarwithy so we left them at Hoarwithy PO to be picked up. We needed chains on the van to cope with winter ice – Capler Lane was the most difficult in bad weather. Major Anderson at Orchard Cottage offered to deliver the Lane in his classic *Rolls Royce* in icy weather. He deducted 10p off his own bill for the service! The round continues today with Nigel Wargen and Kim."

*Sue Clifford née Wargen talking to Madge Daines & Pam Colley 2007*

Nigel and Jill Wargen took over in 1993. The post office business moved here from Manchester House when the Thompsons gave up in 1997.

Bark Cottage 1930s          *J Soulsby*    Norma Massey at work 2006    *Ann Corby*

## Dyers' Haberdashers 1919-29

Annie & Mary E Dyers were dressmakers and haberdashers at Bark House between 1919 and 1929. Their front room was the shop, with buttons, laces, silks, cottons, ribbons, garters and the myriad of little articles that made the old-fashioned haberdashery so fascinating. Mary stayed on at Sunnybank till 1931.

## Waters Ironmongers

Nick & Iris Waters opened a hardware shop next to their home at West Villas in the early 1970s, and sold it to the Yates family in 1983. The business closed in 1988.

## Hair-Dressing

Jocyln Thomas did ladies hairdressing, including trims, shampoos, and permanent waving when she and Geoff took over at The Stores in 1953 though it was not mentioned in the WI survey two years later. Nick & Iris Waters opened a salon at the back of their hardware shop in 1974. Norma Massey joined in 1975 when Margaret Powell & Cheryl Johnson left. The business was bought by Brian Yates in 1983 – Judith joined from Hereford, married his son David. The salon moved to the front when the hardware business closed in 1988.

"It built up customers from a wide area between Hereford, Ross and Ledbury with some from further afield – about a third are men ( was only 5% in early years). Prices have remained very competitive with those of the towns. Services include washes, shampoos, perms, highlights, blow-dries, pedicures (feet!) and Indian head massage.

There were three staff in 2006, Judith Rogers (owner), Norma Massey, and Belinda, each works four days a week.

There are a lot of health and safety checks. The fire extinguisher and hair driers are checked annually. I have been trained to inspect the hands of staff for dermatitis. We even have to pay £100 a year for an entertainment licence so clients can listen to the radio!"

*Judith Rogers & Norma Massey talking to Mandy Dees & Pam Colley 2006*

Fownhope WI collected some shop prices for their 1955 history which are re-produced here with updates, including those produced by the son of one of the authors of that 1955 report. Village shops have survived a 75 fold price rise in the past 118 years – but there's no suggestion that prices in town shops have fared any differently.

| Fownhope Grocery Prices 1889 to 2007 | | | | | | |
|---|---|---|---|---|---|---|
| | Quantity | 1889 | 1928 | 1955 | 1999 | 2007 |
| | | FWI | FWI | FWI | Hilditch | Wargens |
| sugar | Pound | 0.4p | 0.1p | 3.1p | 25p | 40p |
| tea | Quarter | 2.3p | | | 68p | 66p |
| cheese | Pound | 1.25p | | | £2.79 | £2.89 |
| bacon | Pound | 2.5p | | | | £3.38 |
| lard | Pound | 2.9p | | | 36p | 44.5p |
| currants | Pound | 1.25p | | | £4.37 | |
| butter | Pound | 5p | 5p | 30p | £1.72 | £1.62 |
| eggs | Twenty | 5p | 8p | 29p | £2.50 | £2.40 |
| lemon | One | | 0.3p | 2p | 19p | 29p |
| milk | Pint | 0.6p | | | 39p | 36p |
| Retail Price Index | | 19 (1900) | 35 | 80 | 1228 | 1428 (2005) |
| Prices in 'new money' Fownhope WI 1955 – Hilditch update 1999 | | | | | | |

Powell's milk round

*D Bond*

# THE POSTAL SERVICE

Fownhope Post Office, set up by 1846 at Tan House, provided a wide range of services in 1919 – money orders, savings bank, annuity and insurance and telegraph office.  Post arrived from Hereford by 7.45 am, was delivered door-to-door, and dispatched from the office at 5.15 pm.

Hettie Brown                                          *R Brown*

Esther ('Hettie') Bradley had come from Stourbridge in 1897 as assistant, married Arthur Brown a carpenter with Stone Brothers, taken on the post contract, and become something of a legend.

## FOWNHOPE'S POST OFFICE

| location | year | sub-postmaster | services |
|---|---|---|---|
| Tan House | 1906 | Hettie Brown | |
| | 1945 | Alfred C Leney | + pensions |
| | 1952 | Dora Grant | +Girobank 1968 |
| Manchester House | 1970 | Edward (Ted) Pocknell | |
| | 1976 | Anthony & Ann Ball | deliveries by van from Hereford |
| | 1993 | Ann & Anthony Corby | |
| | 1996 | Rob & Angie Thompson | |
| West End Stores | 1997 | Jill & Nigel Wargen | |
| | | *Maxine Williams assistant* | |

Ferry Lane & post office c 1904

*V E Biggs*

### HETTIE BROWN RETIRES 1945

The forthcoming retirement of Mrs. H. Brown as postmistress of Fownhope was marked on Saturday evening by the presentation to her of £44.6s. subscribed by parishioners and friends as a token of esteem and regard for her long and faithful services. Mrs. Brown entered the Fownhope Post Office as assistant to the then postmaster Mr. William Halford 48 years ago on the inauguration of the telegraph service, which was a single wire from Hereford operating a morse code instrument and she sent the first telegram for Mr. Arthur Lechmere, son of the late Mr. Thomas Lechmere of Fownhope Court. On the decease of Mr. Halford and her marriage, Mrs. Brown was appointed postmistress of Fownhope, a position she has now filled for 38 years. All the many changes and improvements in postal work and service, including the telephone, have taken place during her period of office, and her unfailing kindness and sympathy in giving assistance to those not *"au fait"* with various requirements and regulations won for her universal regard. Her retirement causes profound regret but all hope that she and her husband will spend many happy years of restfulness.

*Hereford Times 17 Feb 1945*

There were protests from the Parish Council when the last collection was cut back from 6.15 pm to 5.30 pm in 1953. Sunday collections, abandoned in 1976, were restored at West End Stores in 1990, but ceased in October 2007.

The Common Hill, Fownhope

Common Hill postcard                                                                    *V E Biggs*

(1950s) "We were open from nine to six, an hour for lunch and half day Saturdays. A certain lady used to come in about five minutes to six with parcels for Yorkshire and they would always be delivered the next morning. The counter was open until 10.30 on Christmas morning in case we had any telegrams. Now you won't get that. We've gone backwards not forwards.

At Club Walk we had Billy Watkins' fair. He liked to bank in the post office bank, you see, and he came up Ferry Lane with a wheelbarrow full of silver. Mind he'd got it all in a great big bag and I had to count … it was nearly £500 all in silver but I couldn't do it while the post office was open. I had to do it at night."

*Dora Grant with Pam Colley & Mandy Dees 2006*

The Post office moved again in 1997 from Manchester House to West End Stores. A new postbox was provided at West End – the old box moved east to the Memorial Hall – success at last for the long running campaign for boxes at either end of the village.

### Delivering The Post
Alice Colborn did the round for 24 years from 1919 to 1943. The vicar, Charles Cottrell raised £20 from 200 grateful customers as a tribute to 24 years of service. Two people were needed again when a second delivery was introduced. The village and main road were served by bike round, the outlying area by foot.

1930s "Mrs Colborn lived in one of the four houses where the Garage is now. She moved to Tump Cottage (1935) when they pulled them down. She used to walk down through the woods up by Common Hill, poor girl. She had a whistle for you to go down and fetch your mail because it took such a time going up people's drives from the Pump. She walked with that big bag from Fownhope up the Nash to the Chapel and across the fields down Lea Wood and then out at the corner of Hawkers Lane onto Common Hill. She kept on till she was very old."

*May Meredith née Harrison with Mandy Dees & Janet Jones 2005*

1952 The post came from the sorting office in Hereford in sacks in a van and we sorted into different packs. Alice did the village round from Morney Cross to Capler, cycling five or six days a week

Brenda Broome at Shears Hill did the outside round, nine miles walking including Nash Hill, Fishpool, Lee Wood and the whole of Common Hill. She blew her whistle when she was coming and people would come from their house to collect the mail. There was usually someone at home.

Later my husband Tom Grant was postman for a time, then Edith Joslyn of Morney Cottage who had been a relief postman took over the village round. We did a delivery Christmas morning.

*Dora Grant talking to Mandy Dees & Pam Colley, 2006*

John Newman served as a postman for 33 years from 1946. He cycled into Hereford from his home at Fiddlers Green, caught the bus to Canon Pyon, did an eight hour, 18 mile, round by foot, caught the bus back into town, walked back to the Post Office, and cycled home. He also delivered the post locally in the 1950s as relief for his neighbour Edith Joslyn.

Common Hill postbox & phone *S Gough*

John Newman 1936 *self*

## Delivering The Post 1970-74

"I started work at 6.30am sorting the post at Manchester House, delivered from Morney Cross to Rise Farm, the village, and up Woolhope Road but didn't cover Common Hill or Oldway. After the post I did the school dinners, then worked at Wargens in the afternoon."

*Lilian Thomas talking to Mandy Dees and Pam Colley 2006*

Manchester House 1993          *Ann Corby*

Manchester House 1993          *Ann Corby*

In 1974 two men in little red vans from Hereford took over. Maurice Herman delivered Common Hill and Woolhope for 14 years till 2007.

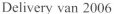
Delivery van 2006          *D M Clark*

Telephone exchange Whiterdine

## Telephones

The phone service was introduced in the mid 1920s, based on Holme Lacy station which served as far as Brockhampton. Dr Baggs and Arthur Powell at Lucksall were connected by 1926. Fownhope had a call office at the Post Office at Tan House by 1929 – *Fownhope 1*. The Fownhope exchange served most of Brockhampton and Woolhope but houses in the north of the parish continued with Holme Lacy numbers. The phone was slow to catch on. Only 20 out of 200 properties were connected by 1941.

| PHONE SUBSCRIBERS 1941 | | |
|---|---|---|
| Godfrey Malkin, doctor | Mona | *F 35* |
| Arthur Powell, timber merchant | Lucksall | *H L 13* |
| Edmund Lechmere | Fownhope Court | *F 37* |
| James Thairs, publican | Green Man | *F 43* |
| Lloyd James, grocer | The Stores | *F 42* |
| Edmund Gange, art critic | The Folly | *F 26* |
| Richard Dane | Morney Cross | *F 38* |
| Mabel Fox | Orchard Cottage | *F 24* |
| Arthur Leslie-Tompson | White Gate | *F 29* |
| Harry Townsend, contractor | Fairfield | *F 47* |
| Misses St Barbe | Whiterdine | *F 23* |
| Kathleen de Winton | Rock House | *F 33* |
| Matthew Leyman, market garden | Stone House | *F 61* |
| Mrs Marshall | Common Hill House | *F 23* |
| Cyril Shelton | Lower House | *F 39* |
| Harry Pugh, publican | Anchor Inn | *H L 24* |
| Hettie Brown, post office | Tan House | *F 34* |
| William Dawe, farmer | Ringfield | *F 62* |
| Edward Hancorn, grocer | Manchester House | *F 20* |
| Edwin Pritchard, butcher | Walworth House | *F 36* |
| Total | | 20 (23) |
| *plus 3 subscribers in Woolhope, 2 in Brockhampton* | | |

The Fownhope code was dropped in 1984, replaced by the 0432 77 *prefix*, which in turn was replaced in 1990 by the 0432 860 *code*, now 01432. The exchange remains next to Whiterdine.

# PUBLIC HOUSES

Fownhope had four pubs in 1919 – a sharp reduction on the 11 pubs and cider houses here in 1841. They played an important part in the social life of the village, even when the Memorial Hall provided an alternative venue for meetings.

| SOME of the PUBLICANS *(some dates approx.)* |
| --- |
| GREEN MAN Esther Samuel 1913-26, Bernard Wall 1926-30, James Thair 1930-46, Harry Fagg 1946-9, Joseph Nicholls 1949-54, Ossie Edwards 1955-79, Arthur Williams 1984-2002 |
| NEW INN Fred Goode 1919-25, William & Lilian White 1926-34, Chas Edwards 1934-41, Geoff Longman 1941-63, Les Gummery 1963-2002, Martin & Sandra Teague 2002- |
| HIGHLAND HOME Jane Williams /Welling 1900-34, James Williams 1919-36, Teresa Williams/Thomas 1921-46, Arthur Thomas 1946-52, Lavinia Harrison 1958-64, Bernard Newton 1975-87, closed 2001 |
| ANCHOR INN *(tenants)* Walter Brown 1910-21, Wallace Shock 1921-25, Herbert Pittaway 1928-46 *(free house 1937)*, Harry & Eunice Pugh 1941-63, Emily Powell 1963-67, closed 1972 |

Green Man interior 2006

*S Gough*

**The Green Man** dates back to the 15th century and served as meeting place, magistrates court, and auction room for centuries. Esther Samuel, continued the Connop family link with the pub. James Thair saw the tourist potential and had 8 bedrooms to let in the 1930s. Harry Fagg, from Oxfordshire, bought the pub in 1945 for £6,500 and managed to combine the role of publican with that of district councillor and captain of the fire brigade. Joseph Nicholls, a Hereford estate agent, made some changes about 1949. Ossie Edwards added some black and white timbering to cover the brick façade, as well as creating extra bedrooms. The hotel earned a *Michelin* recommendation in the 1980s. Arthur Williams added a leisure centre which he retained when he sold the Green Man in 2002.

Green Man                                    *J Soulsby*

Green Man 1993                        *Ann Corby*

**The Highland Home** had been re-built as a beerhouse on Ferry Lane by James Mayo in 1872. His daughter Jane Williams, later Welling, carried on from 1900 to 1934, sharing the business with her son James Williams (1919-1936) and daughter Teresa (1921-1946) who married the wheelwright Arthur Thomas, and shared the business with him briefly. Arthur carried on his own till 1952. There were many licensees after 1953. The name was changed to the Flamenco in1965, and again to the Forge and Ferry in 1973. There were several threats of closure before it finally closed its doors in 2001, to revert to residential use.

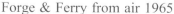
Forge & Ferry from air 1965        *Sky*

Forge & Ferry 2006                    *M Clark*

Mr & Mrs Parrish were a friendly couple. He was small and she was large. They liked to visit the Highland Home on Ferry Lane. Sometimes Mr Parrish would be seen pushing his wife home up the Woolhope Road in a wheelbarrow!

*lived at Nupend Cottage   Wilf Chignell's memoirs 1956*

---

### Highland Home Inn Sale 1952

Greenlands Ltd. Situate in the centre of this picturesque Herefordshire village in a district renowned for its excellent salmon and trout fishing in the Wye and the Inn being a favoured rendezvous for visiting fishermen from a wide area.. Owner-occupier retiring. sale by auction

The Highland Home Inn. Excellent public and smoke room bars, barrel room and server, popular local and Burton beers drawn straight from the wood; comfortable private sitting room, kitchenette, larder and three excellent bedrooms; basement cellarage. Mains electricity, unfailing well water supply.

Outside: ladies and gents conveniences and a large galvanised iron outbuilding suitable for garage. Extensive pull-in and garden, in all estimated to contain a total of just under half an acre. Immediate vacant possession.

Adjoining comfortable cottage residence subject to the weekly tenancy of Mr. H. Chadney at 6s.p.w. (tenant paying rates).

**sold to Mr Stringer of Cheltenham at £4,000**

*Hereford Times Nov/Dec 1952*

---

New Inn 2006                  *M Clark*

New Inn crib game                  *S Gough*

**New Inn** The name may be new but Phelps's beerhouse stood here in 1841. Fred Goode was a carrier by day. William White developed accommodation for tourists and anglers in the 1930s.

Charles Edwards built a bowling green shortly after.  Geoff Longman and Les Gummery served here for 61 years between them.

Magistrates granted a wine licence to the New Inn … petition signed by 125 people supported by Rev W R Chignell, Vicar

*Hereford Times, March 1953*

'To see that licensing laws were kept I'd go and stand outside the pubs at ten o clock, you'd have 20 or 30 in the small room of the New Inn.  If they knew you were outside the pub would be cleared in five or ten minutes and no problems.'

*Phil Paton PC 1952-58, talking to Madge Daines & Pam Colley 2006*

Anchor Inn 1950s  *Michael Williams*

**The Anchor Inn** had close connections with the river trade and the Wheatstone family, and was well used by folk from Holme Lacy which was kept strictly 'dry' by the squires at the big house. Walter Brown was tenant of the Hereford Brewery from 1910. The pub was sold to the county council in 1972 and demolished as part of road improvements at the Holme Lacy bridge junction.

71

# CRAFTS and TRADES

If you lived in the village in 1919 then you worked here too. Only a handful went outside to work – to the railway at Holme Lacy, or a few people rode by bike or horse into Hereford. The range of crafts included:–

## Cobblers

The long-established shoemaking industry based on the tanneries which used local hides, lime and bark, had died out by 1919. The last of the shoemakers, Charlie Brookes on Common Hill, was 77. There were still two cobblers repairing shoes at the time of the WI survey in 1955.

*George Taylor Cobbler 1950s*
"Dad had polio, and had to walk with a caliper. He learnt the trade of shoe repairing in Oswestry Hospital – and repaired shoes for Fownhope and Woolhope from home in Nupend. He charged from 2s 6d *(12.5p)* to 8s 6d *(42.5p)* for repairs. We children delivered the shoes back to customers, and went by bus or bike to Hereford to buy leather etc for Dad."

*Bill Taylor talking to Pam Colley & Madge Daines 2007*

Charlie Brookes 1920s     *J Soulsby*     Powell's coal                    *P Green*

## Coal Merchants

Arthur Powell, *'coal, timber, coke & anthracite merchants'* had coal yards at Holme Lacy station and at Lucksall where he also operated the steam saw mills and made gates, ladders, hurdles and fork handles. Arthur was succeeded by his sons Fred and Victor who handed on to Gerald in 1986. The business declined with the arrival of mains gas in 1991, and closed in 2001. George Biggs was agent for the Phoenix coal company at West Villa and Holme Lacy station where George was also station-master. The business survived till the railway closed in the early 1960s.

Phoenix coal                                                    *M Dees*

## Blacksmiths

Arthur Thomas was at The Forge next to Manchester House from 1914 to 1926. He bought the wheelwright's shop on Ferry Lane in 1926.

Cedric (Sonny) took over in 1964 and replaced the old buildings in 1966. George Thomas joined his father in 1965 when still shod working horses used for forestry work. CG Thomas and Son advertised in 1974 as *'agricultural smiths, doing welding, body builders, gates and fencing of all kinds'*.

Thomas at Forge 1960s          *R Thomas*

Thomas at Forge 1960s          *R Thomas*

73

Cedric George 'Sonny' Thomas worked at the Forge in Ferry Lane with his father *(Arthur James Thomas)* in the 1940s, stayed there when he married Rene. Father remarried and moved out.

Sonny got up 6.45am, drank four cups of tea to think out the day's work, worked before breakfast at 8.30am. He shod horses, made gates, trailers, muck spreaders for farmers, and did welding.

Clifford George Thomas joined Sonny having worked for Len Evans at Canon Pyon. Other staff included Alec Rivenski, Polish evacuee, carpenter, and Cyril Rogers from Woolhope, who did odd jobs. We also rented the smithy at Mordiford from Major Hereford which operated once a week. Sonny's father and grandfather had worked there.

*Rene Thomas talked to Madge Daines & Pam Colley 2006*

George Thomas employed two men in 1997, working in steel, to manufacture trailers, gates, ornamental work and repairs to farm equipment. They made a fairground carousel that went on tour in Malaysia, and a horse weighing platform which helped to win gold for the Australians at the Atlanta Olympics.

### The Motor Trade

Fownhope's first repair business was started by the sons of the parish clerk. Donald Jones hired out cars and sold a range of oils in 1923 from 'Highlands Garage' opposite the Church. By 1926 Jones Brothers were listed as motor engineers. The brothers stayed in the village until 1946 but are not listed in the directories after 1929 so the business may not have thrived.

West End pumps 1959          *N Cope*   Fownhope Motors 2006          *M Clark*

Edwin F Godsell lived at Highland Place from 1934 to 1973, before moving to Nover Wood where he stayed till 1983. He started his business in Fairfield Green before the new garage replaced some picturesque hovels, including the Round House next to Tanhouse by 1947 where he offered *'service, petrol, diesel, oils, tyres and accessories, cars and coach hire'*. He was selling cars by 1956. He was still in business in 1981 as Godsell's garage. The business was sold to Peter Nash, trading as Fownhope Motors and as Mitsubishi agents. Petrol sales ceased in 2005.


### Biggs Motors 1952-1993

Denzil Biggs from Lechmere Ley became an apprentice motor mechanic in Hereford, and set up his own repair business in 1952 in a building behind The Stores ( now Cassiobury). He took on help later from Ray Evans, Nigel Davies, Roger Moss, and John Jones as an apprentice. He moved his business in 1958 to his father's Dutch barn behind Ringfield. Biggs did body repairs and re-sprays, MoT tests and sold petrol and oils. A new workshop was built in 1975. Denzil retired in 1993 – the 'brownfield' site was sold for new housing. John Jones went to work for Fownhope Motors. Roger Moss set up his own repair business including MoTs at Upper Littlehope Farm.

Biggs garage Ringfield          *D Biggs*   Biggs garage Ringfield          *D Biggs*


In 1958 my mother and father bought Ringfield, it was on market for quite a long time. I'd outgrown the old shed – there used to be a lot of vehicles parked on the road opposite the school, so there was no difficulty getting permission to move ( the garage business) to Ringfield barn. It was a good business. We lived well on it. Never made any money. I enjoyed doing work – it was a good life.

*Denzil Biggs talking to Pam Colley & Madge Daines 2006*


### Fownhope Pottery 1958-63

Denis Lacey set up his pottery at Nupend Mill, now Viltis, in 1958 and lived at Mill Cottage with Edith to 1963 when he moved the business to Fromes Hill on the Worcester road where the 'Fownhope Pottery' sign is still clear, though Dennis has retired to Ceredigion.

Dennis Lacey at pottery 1959                                    *self*

## Tourist Trade

Fownhope has drawn tourists to enjoy the countryside and 'picturesque' Wye Valley views since the late 18th century. The Green Man had long catered for tourists, and was joined by the New Inn in 1931. Grace Warren at Joans Hill Farm offered full board to tourists in the 1967 farm holiday guide. Tan House provided bed and breakfast accommodation by 1976, followed by Bowens in 1980, Bark Cottage, Oaklands and Pippins by 1998.

Pippins B&B                     *A Corby*   Pippins B&B                   *A Corby*

Several properties have also been used as self-catering holiday accommodation including Fern Cottage, Chapel Cottage on Ferry Lane (complete with outdoor swimming pool), and the Coach House at Whiterdine.

## Lucksall Caravans

Lucksall Caravan and Camping Park was started in 1978 by Vic Powell on land adjacent to his coal yard. The business was sold by his son Gerald Powell to Gary and Deborah Williams in 2003 who employ five staff including managers Alan and Karen Matthews. The site, open from March to the end of November, includes 80 pitches, and 10 static vans, and an adjacent rally field as well as a shop opened in 2005.

Lucksall caravans 1990s   *G Powell*   Lucksall caravans 1990s   *G Powell*

**Bowens** farmhouse was converted by Amy Williams in 1980 as a guest house, and featured on the *BBC Holiday* programme in 1982. Carol Hart bought the business in 1983 –

Oaklands B&B   *S Clifford*   The Bowens Guest House 2006   *D M Clark*

77

"I have made many improvements, including converting outbuildings. We have ten *en suite* bedrooms *(2 less than in 1993)*, including four at ground floor, draw tourist and business guests through the year as well as functions in the restaurant. Tourists tend to be older guests who enjoy walking and sight-seeing. Bowens has had recommendations from *Michelin* and from Paddy Burt in the *Telegraph*. We source our vegetables and meat locally, employ 10 part and full-time staff, many more than it did as a working farm."

*Carol Hart talking to Mandy Dees & Pam Colley, 2007*

## Leisure Centre

Wye Leisure was opened in June 1999 by the Williams family, partly as a facility for guests at the *Green Man*, and for local members. It started with four staff, and 250 members with a swimming pool, spa pool, sauna, steam room, gymnasium and beauty salon. The club was fully subscribed within six months, and facilities were doubled in February 2001 with the addition of a coffee shop. More land was acquired at the rear of Fownhope Motors for a further extension in early 2006. This extended facilities to 3 pools, 4 saunas, 3 steam rooms, 4 spas, an outdoor spa, improved changing rooms, coffee shop, computers with internet access, beauty salons, as well as a new restaurant. The centre now employs 45 people *(compared with 4 in 1999)* with 8000 club members from a wide area.

Wye leisure from air 2002     *J Jones*     Leisure Centre & Court 2006     *M Clark*

## Commuting

The bus made it possible to work in Hereford. In the war years many people worked at the ordnance factory at Rotherwas.

We were on shifts, three shifts. I worked with cordite, sometimes it was little bits of cordite and sometimes longer cordite that you had to tie. It was to go inside a brass shell and something else was to go in it from the South side. The factory was divided into two very different parts and I was on the North side. They used powder which made their clothes and everything go yellow on the South side, but our side was clean. We had to wear hats and thick overalls. We were mainly women in our department but there were men taking away the boxes. The railway ran through the factory. Hundreds were employed and people used to come from the Forest of Dean and miles out. ... I came then to live at Lucksall and went onto all 'days'. I used to catch the bus by the Anchor Inn ... It was a special bus and a lot of people came from Fownhope. I was there when the bomb was dropped in the morning. We were in the air-raid shelters. But the bomb dropped on the South side and I was on the North side. ... I think that airplane was really low ... I think it was just a stray one. I can remember when there was a 2,000 lb bomb that over-heated on the South side. I think we were not allowed in until it was made safe. Brian Chamberlain's father was a fireman at the factory.

*Doris Bond née Powell with Pam Colley & Madge Daines, 2005*

Many people travelled by bus to Hereford in the 1950s and the car ownership brought more 'commuters'. By 1971 over the half the population (52%) worked outside the rural district area. This rose to 71% in the 1981 census. The *Parish Plan survey* in 2003 concluded that most of the workforce (54%) commuted between 5 and 15 miles, i.e. to places such as Hereford, but there were 17% who travelled more than 15 miles, some more than 40 miles each day.

Fownhope is much more than a mere dormitory. Fownhope may not have struck oil but new businesses such as the Leisure Centre and the Medical Centre mean that more people work in Fownhope in 2005 than was the case in 1919 even though many residents now work elsewhere.

The other big change has been the rise in home-work. One in seven of Fownhope's workforce worked from home in 2001 – that's 58 people. *That compares with only 10 in 1981.* There's Ken Pearce painter and decorator, David Yates, carpenter, William Dereham, an IT expert, Peter Martin, an architect, Andrew Pearce, landscape gardener, Steve Chandler, the builder, Ann Corby's airport taxi service, and many more.

# ROADS

Road surfaces in 1919 were uneven, rutted, potholed, puddled and dusty in dry weather. Repairs were little more than filling the cracks with loose stones though steam rollers were used to compress Clee Hill stone. Drainage had improved since the 1890s.

Ferry Lane                                                            *T Ely / J Soulsby*

The Parish Council campaigned to get local roads *'tar-sprayed'*. The county surveyor, GH Jack had argued that the tar from Hereford gasworks tar was too soluble – country lanes needed to be re-built first. The main road from the city to Mordiford however was tarred by 1921 with a material known as *asphalnac* on limestone (from a new depot at Scutterine Quarry), and this was extended to Fownhope at a cost of £2800 between 1922 and 1928, though the route by Nash Pitch to Old Gore had to wait. Other roads were '*surface dressed*' – a scattering of tar to reduce dust levels. The county surveyor took over responsibility for the minor roads in 1930, and was critical

| | |
|---|---|
| *C295 Woolhope Road* | Foundation fair, surface poor, hedges and ditches fair |
| *U632 Common Hill Lane* | Steep and narrow, foundation and surface very rough |
| *C273 Oldstone Lane* | narrow steep lane, very rough and bad |

Cycle traffic had overtaken the horse by the time of the first traffic census in 1923, and was particularly heavy on market days and at weekends as people rode out from Hereford. But in the next six years motor traffic doubled to take over from all over forms of transport

|  | Horse ridden | Horse drawn | Pedal cycles | Motor vehicles |
|---|---|---|---|---|
| 1923 | 107 | 457 | 1828 | 1067 |
| 1929 | 39 | 247 | 1330 | 1954 |
|  | County surveyors 7 day census on the main road | | | |

Main road 1919                *V E Biggs*

Tump Cottage 1919                *V E Biggs*

The Parish Council asked for a 30 mph speed limit through the village in 1935 as road surfaces improved. George Wood, worked on the roads as a lengthsman in the 1930s, clearing ditches, removing debris, and filling potholes. He was followed by Dickie Brookes who lived at The Folly on Common Hill whose work is remembered with affection

Common Hill Lane was in far better order than now because Dickie Brookes was the road man and it was immaculate. It was a third wider than it is now, and never had any puddles – *Joan Hill 2005*

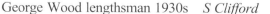

George Wood lengthsman 1930s   *S Clifford*

Marjorie Davies cyclist 1930s   *S Clifford*

Roadbuilding 1918                                                                 *HRO*

## Holme Lacy Bridge

Fownhope people had been reluctant to invest in the private toll-bridge back in 1856, but the Parish Council tried to persuade the County Council to buy the bridge. Shareholders cannot have been too impressed with their annual dividends of 1% but it took till 1936 for the company to sell for £725, just in time for the council to replace the buckled steel decking with concrete girders in 1937. The bridge was still too narrow but we had to wait till 1973 for the council, facing merger with Worcestershire, to build a new steel three span bridge with re-inforced concrete slabs.

Holme Lacy bridge toll 1930    *S Clifford*   In flood                      *J Soulsby*

(1930s) "You had to pay a penny to walk over the bridge.
My father Arthur Powell was the timber and coal merchant at Lucksall. He hauled timber to Holme Lacy station, it was fourpence for the horse and

82

cart. He had an account, it would be two or three pound, that would be a lot of money. The lady, a war widow with six children, lived in the little toll-house, opening and closing the gate for people to go through."

*Mabel Williams (née Powell) 2005*

Early Car  A Wood               *D Brown*

Chauffeur               *D Brown*

## Cycling

Cycling had its share of dangers or thrills –

(1951) "I used to start at the top of Tump Pitch and cycle down. The ladies at Orchard Cottage, Mrs Fox and Miss Duncomb, rang my mother at Tump Farm and said, *'Are you aware of what your daughter's doing?'* On one occasion I went into the brook outside the butcher's shop full of sewerage and I came out coated from head to toe! Mrs Leyman from Stone House kindly took me to her house and bathed me and brought me home."

*Jennifer Higham (née Williams), with Mandy Dees & Pam Colley, 2005*

Car ownership increased quite dramatically from the 1960s. By 1971 76% of households in the parish owned cars. This increased to 86% in 2001 census, and with it the proportion of households with two or more cars rose from 21% to 37%. The actual number of cars owned in the parish trebled from 200 in 1971 to 630 in 2001.

## Increasing Traffic

"The build up of traffic has been enormous in the last ten years. Thirty years ago we often drove cattle or sheep along the B4224 between Buckenhill and How Caple for three miles, now it is impossible.
Traffic also runs too fast. Speed limits are not enforced and are largely ignored."

*John Edwards of How Caple, county council chairman Feb 2007*

Following several serious accidents including one outside Oldway Chapel, the BADD group was formed in 1993 to highlight safety problems on the road between Upton Bishop and Hampton Bishop, and get action to reduce traffic speed, improve the carriage-way and traffic signs, impose weight limits, and raise driving standards

Village 'gateway' 1996    *J Hardwick*

Holme Lacy new bridge 2007    *D M Clark*

A petition, signed by 500 residents, and a public meeting attended by over a hundred people in the Memorial Hall pressed for action. The council responded with warning signs and speed limits, though BAD's chairman, John Watson, felt that the county council's response was inadequate given the additional traffic using the road to get to the expanding industrial estate at Rotherwas

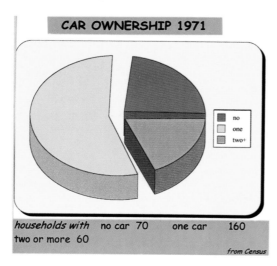
CAR OWNERSHIP 1971

no
one
two+

households with    no car 70      one car      160
two or more 60

*from Census*

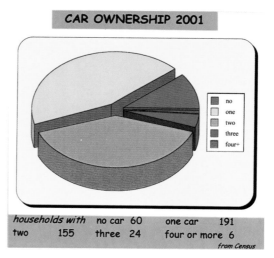
CAR OWNERSHIP 2001

no
one
two
three
four+

households with    no car 60      one car      191
two        155      three 24      four or more 6

*from Census*

84

# THE BUS SERVICE

Fownhope's horse-drawn carrier had provided a return trip to Hereford on market days since the 1840s – a social event celebrated in verse. However the motor bus did not arrive until 1920 – twenty years after the city. *Birmingham and Midland Red's* trial service in March 1920 ran on Wednesdays and Saturdays from Hereford to Fownhope by Mordiford. It must have been so much easier than taking the horse-drawn cart, or walking to Holme Lacy station. The service generated frenzied excitement in the local press

Herefordshire people welcomed the 'Red' motor bus invasion on Wednesday in no half-hearted fashion. As expected, the Birmingham and Midland Company's buses attracted widespread attention. They arrived at short notice. An addition to the printed timetable was made for a 9am 'bus runs from Fownhope to Hereford on Wednesday and Saturday. The present arrangements are purely experimental...the loads that came into the city to do their marketing gave ample proof of the long felt need for road transport
These red 'buses seat 29 passengers, and can accommodate 35 passengers with ease. They are light running and comfortable, and have 40-h.p. petrol-electric engines, which enable the vehicle to start with a gliding motion and run up hill. The cost of one of these 'buses is £2,000.

*Hereford Times 1920*

By June 1921 *Midland Red's* buses ran daily with extras on Wednesdays and Saturdays and a Saturday evening service from Hereford at 9.30pm. By the late 1926 services were extended through Old Gore to Ross, and to Woolhope.

*Midland Red* drew rivals. Mrs Capper adapted an old farm vehicle which ran across country from St Weonards by Brockhampton to Fownhope and Hereford. She offered lower fares without frills – on one trip passengers shared with nine eight year old pigs on single tickets to Hereford market!

(1930s) "8.15 bus in morning to get to school in Hereford, bus back in the morning at 10.30am for shoppers, one at mid-day, another brought us back from school about 4.30pm. Later on it got more civilised there was a late bus at 6.15pm for people who worked in the shops. On Saturday a very late bus at 10.30pm used to go right through to Woolhope."
*Harry Robbins at Rudge End talking to Janet & Ian Jones 2006*

Bus services, reduced during the war years to save fuel were restored and extended in 1948.

> Service No. 466/7 – Hereford, Fownhope and Woolhope
> **Weekdays**
> The 1.5 p.m. Hereford to Fownhope will run through to Woolhope.New journey, Woolhope to Hereford at 1.45 p.m., replacing the 1.33 p.m. Fownhope to Hereford
> The 4.30 p.m. Hereford to Woolhope (Mons. to Fridays) will
> leave at 4.35 p.m. and connect at Fownhope with the bus from Ross-on-Wye.
> **Wednesdays.**
> New journey leaving Hereford for Fownhope at 9.0pm, returning at 9.25pm
> **Saturdays**
> New journey leaving Hereford for Woolhope at 9.0pm, returning at 9.40pm
>
> *Hereford Times 1948*

The improved bus service made it possible to work in town :
*(1949) I worked at Greenlands in Hereford. The bus picked up at Church Cross and the Green Man. The buses weren't too frequent and they got very crowded. I had to walk to the bus station from High Town to be sure of getting a seat.*

*Jean Phillips talking to Mandy Dees & Pam Colley 2005*

Services peaked in the 1950s with 81 trips per week in 1957 into Hereford, more than double the pre-war numbers. The return fare to Hereford was 1s 5d in 1955. *Midland Red* ran all the services, including runs to Hereford by Holme Lacy. Extra buses ran on Wednesday and Saturday, including a 10.35pm return, and three on Sundays, extending into the evening. There was an early morning service to Ross, and a Saturday evening bus returning from Ross at 10.50pm. Early bus services had been geared towards the demands of shoppers to get to Hereford on Wednesday and Saturdays. By the 1950s services were more evenly spread to satisfy the needs of people working and studying in Hereford, and for entertainment. But a parish meeting in 1952 rejected calls for a bus shelter to serve the new estate at Court Orchard (denied again in 1972) though a year later the new lychgate was built as a bus shelter to serve the east end of the village.

## BUSES – THE BEST YEARS – 1957

*The bus service reached its peak around 1957 – there were more buses, you could work in town, shop in Ross, and spend an evening in town, even on a Sunday.*

| | | 1920 | 1957 | 1980 | 2007 |
|---|---|---|---|---|---|
| to Hereford | *Number weekly* | 17 | 81 | 29 | 62 |
| | *Early bus to work* | no | 7am | 8.05 am | 7.11 am |
| | *Work Rotherwas* | no | 7am | no | no |
| night out | *Weekdays (back)* | no | 9.45pm | none | |
| | *Sat* | 9.30 pm | 10.35 | no | |
| Sunday service | | 2 *inc* 6.15 pm | 3 *inc* 9.15 pm | no | no |
| to Ross | *to shop* | no | 1 daily | no | no |
| *Sat evening* | | no | 10.50 pm | no | no |

## Decline 1960-80

Bus service levels were cut in 1957 as a response to fuel shortage (Suez crisis) and were not restored later. Passenger numbers fell during the 1960s as more people got their own car. Fownhope services, losing £5,000 a year in 1976, were kept going by the profits from Midland Red's town services. South Herefordshire Council did not bring in a concessionary scheme to help their pensioners with travel costs until 1979, offering only £2.50 worth of tokens.

By 1980 Midland Red passed local routes to another company:

G H Yeomans. Greystones Coaches started a shoppers bus in 1980 on Tuesdays from Mordiford by Fownhope to Newent and Gloucester. A former bus driver from Newent, known, as 'Flash' Whitehead ran another service in 1977 from Newent on Wednesdays and Saturdays through Fownhope to Hereford.

## Fownhope on Trial 1981-83

Fownhope was included in the County Council's *'trial area'* in 1981 to encourage new services and reduce subsidy costs. Flashes Coaches took over from Yeomans, much against the wishes of the Parish Council who objected to the change of operator and timetable. Within a month the county council had received a flood of complaints about Flashes' operation. The buses were old and dirty, pick up points in Hereford change without notice, times change without warning, buses fail to arrive, fail to keep time; skipped bus stops, and broke down, with no replacement provided. The complaints continued. Flash used a private car to convey passengers, failed to complete journeys, and failed to pay for taxis taken when no service was provided. The bus was parked in a layby overnight. Buses were crowded with standing room only.

The County officers recorded three days in October 1982

*Monday 25th* vehicle failure – repairer didn't arrive till 14.35
*Tuesday 26h* breakdown – passengers carried in Mr Whitehead's car
*Wed 27th* did not run – no vehicle

The Commissioners inspected Flashes vehicles to find a missing shock absorber, tyres worn below the legal limit, and worn brake linings. They revoked his licence in February 1983, and the county council cancelled Flashes contract.

Bus  Court Orchard 2007                                                                 *D M Clark*

## More Services Under Rural Bus Grant 1998

The return of a Herefordshire Council in 1998, coincided with new rural bus grants which increased services from 46 to 62 buses a week to Hereford. A summer Sunday service was re-introduced to Hereford and Ross which ran for six summers till 2003. But a shopper bus on Thursdays to Ross only lasted two years.

# TRAINS

Holme Lacy station, some three miles from Fownhope across the toll bridge, offered a worthy service in the 1920s of eight trains each day to Hereford, Ross and Gloucester, with scope for trips to London's Paddington station. The goods yard was used by Fownhope's coal merchants, the builders, Stone Brothers, and by the Forestry Commission for their Haugh Wood operations after 1925.

Holme Lacy station 1959 *N Cope*

| GWR Train Timetable 1939 | | | | | | | | | |
|---|---|---|---|---|---|---|---|---|---|
| Hereford | 7.05 | 7.35 | 10.20 | 1.15 | 2.20 | 4.10 | 6.48 | 8.55 | 9.35 |
| **Holme Lacy** | **7.13** | **7.43** | **10.28** | **1.23** | **2.28** | **4.18** | **6.56** | **9.04** | **9.43** |
| Ross | 7.27 | 8.01 | 10.47 | 1.44 | 2.46 | 4.36 | 7.19 | 9.20 | 10.01 |
| Gloucester | 8.06 | 8.46 | 11.31 | 2.25 | 3.25 | 5.17 | 8.02 | 10.08 | 10.42 |
| | | | | | | | | *exc sat* | *sat only* |
| Gloucester | 7.15 | 9.45 | 12.35 | 2.05 | 3.47 | 6.10 | 9.24 | | |
| Ross | 8.05 | 10.27 | 1.20 | 2.48 | 4.35 | 6.54 | 10.03 | | |
| **Holme Lacy** | **8.26** | **10.49** | **1.44** | **3.09** | **4.57** | **7.17** | **10.20** | | |
| Hereford | 8.33 | 10.57 | 1.51 | 3.16 | 5.04 | 7.24 | 10.30 | | |

*GWR summer timetable – Kevin Gough*

(1940s) "My uncle George Biggs was stationmaster at Holme Lacy. He and Lionel used to run a coal business there as well. When we were quite young we'd take Dad's pony and the trolley (a four-wheel truck) over the toll-bridge and deliver coal around Holme Lacy, and he'd give us a couple of bob. George lived at West Villas and cycled to Holme Lacy station. When we lived at Lechmere Ley you could time the trains – *"there's the half past eight gone down."*

*Denzil Biggs, with Madge Daines & Pam Colley, 2006*

The line was expensive to maintain, involved several awkward tunnels and bridges, with few potential passengers in the villages between Holme Lacy and Ross. Strangford bridge collapsed in the floods of March 1947. The service did not improve after nationalization though it was still possible to reach London by 10.35am in 1960.

| British Rail Train Timetable 1963 | | | | | | | | | |
|---|---|---|---|---|---|---|---|---|---|
| Hereford | 6.55 | 7.32 | 10.25 | 1.40 | 2.43 | 4.30 | 6.02 | 9.05 | 9.42 |
| **Holme Lacy** | **7.04** | **7.41** | **10.34** | **1.49** | **2.52** | **4.39** | **6.15** | **9.14** | **9.50** |
| Ross | 7.20 | 7.59 | 10.56 | 2.07 | 3.10 | 4.57 | 6.34 | 9.32 | 10.11 |
| Gloucester | 8.02 | 8.46 | 11.38 | 2.49 | 3.58 | 5.47 | 7.18 | 10.16 | 10.57 |
| | | | | *ex sat* | | | | *exc sat* | *sat only* |
| Gloucester | 7.00 | 9.50 | 12.25 | 2.30 | 4.08 | 5.56 | 7.36 | 10.00 | 10.17 |
| Ross | 7.45 | 10.31 | 1.04 | 3.09 | 4.48 | 6.32 | 8.13 | 10.40 | 10.57 |
| **Holme Lacy** | **8.27** | **10.55** | **1.33** | **3.33** | **5.21** | **6.58** | **8.37** | **11.01** | **11.23** |
| Hereford | 8.37 | 11.04 | 1.42 | 3.46 | 5.30 | 7.07 | 8.46 | 11.10 | 11.32 |
| | | | | | | | *sat only* | *exc sat* | *sat only* |

*source ABC Guide June 1963*

Nevertheless it was a sad day when the line closed in 1964 as part of the Beeching cuts. The Parish Council had protested but then reversed its stance as the *'parish is not directly concerned'* but then asked (*without success*) for any replacement bus between Hereford and Gloucester to run through Fownhope or connect at Ross.

# HEALTH & WELFARE

| Fownhope's Doctors | | |
|---|---|---|
| 1919-39 | Dr James C Baggs | Mona |
| 1923-25 | Dr Lionel Dene Lowsley | |
| 1939-65 | Dr Godfrey Malkin | |
| 1963-96 | Dr Patrick Ramage | |
| 1990 on | Dr Christopher Allen | |
| 1994-96 | Dr Shirley Davies | Medical Centre, Island Orchard |
| 1996 on | Dr Alison Wood | |
| 2000 on | Dr Michael Hearne | |
| 2004 on | Dr Heather King | |

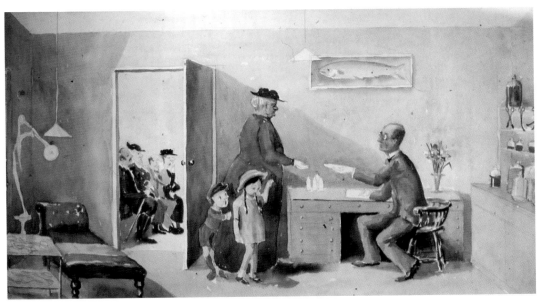

Surgery 1930s – artistic licence

*Pip Leyman*

Fownhope has had a resident doctor since the 18th century. Dr **James Baggs**, who took over from Dr Thompson in 1919, was the son of a Portsmouth publican, remembered as a smoker, and for his colourful language and short-temper. Mona on Capler Lane was his home and surgery. He was a keen fisherman and employed a ghyllie. He co-founded the Legion branch, and went back to naval service for two years, when **Lionel Lowsley** came here from London. Dr Lowsley brought in Stone Brothers to make some improvements to the house in 1923.

"Dr Baggs was a naval doctor, and could be a bit gruff. We had ringworms, and paid 7s 6d *(37.5p)* to see Dr Baggs. Father was only paid 30s a week in those days. We had to see him the morning of the Club Walk – '*Can't you pick a better time?*' He didn't drive but had his own chauffeur."

*Phyllis Yarranton née Alford talking to Mandy Dees & Pam Colley 2006*

Dr Baggs ran branch surgeries in Woolhope, Ballingham and Brockhampton *(Ladyridge Farm)* from the 1930s. Facilities were limited and patients had to get any drugs from the surgery in Fownhope. Woolhope's surgery in the vicarage dated from before 1895 when Dr Averay Jones provided medicines for the subscribers to the Woolhope Dispensary. Branch surgeries had closed by the time Patrick Ramage took over in 1965.

Dr Baggs 1933                           *N Cope*

Dr Malkin's rounds 1953                *N Cope*

The **Fownhope Nursing Association** was set up in 1920 to employ a trained nurse to serve Fownhope, Mordiford and Woolhope. One of the founders was the retired doctor, Edgar Averay Jones at Stone House, who argued that "*hitherto they had skilled village women, but not certificated. There was a general feeling that something more than the nurses of the Sarah Gamp type was wanted.*" The salaries – laid down by the Hereford Board of Guardians were £45 for less than one year's service, over two years £50. One of the first was Mrs Annie Morris, listed as the *midwife* at Yew Tree Cottage *(now Oaklands)* in 1929, who moved to Whiterdine, and then to The Green.

Reginald Jones ran a branch dental surgery in Fern House once a week in the late 1930s from his surgeries in Ledbury and Hereford. He presumably brought most of his equipment with him each week. The service didn't survive after the war.

Dr Baggs continued the tradition of single-handed doctors in the village, but was helped from time to time by young doctors getting experience of rural practice. Godfrey Malkin, from North Staffordshire, came here for a short spell in 1931, and came back when James Baggs retired in 1939. Godfrey, a keen naturalist and photographer, contributed much to the community for the next three decades, not simply as doctor, but as chairman of the Parish Council and numerous committees.

Dr Malkin's surgery 1951          *N Cope*   Dr Malkin's surgery 1951          *N Cope*

I remember paying Dr Malkin for the medical treatment when our children were young. They had measles quite badly and it was quite expensive. But straight after that the NHS came in and that covered the costs
*Mabel Williams née Powell with Madge Daines & Pam Colley 2005*

My mother used to clean the Surgery at Mona. I used to get Dr Malkin's breakfast and then he'd go into the surgery. I looked after his little girl

Neenie, and helped with the general work. All the bottles were underneath the bench in the little waiting room.

*Dorothy Crowe née Pocknell with Pam Colley & Madge Daines 2005*

The waiting room at Mona was very small. We sat on benches. There were big jars on the shelves above. Dr Malkin's room was comfy and warm. He made his own medicines. We always went away with a tonic! (1950s).

*Jean Phillips talking to Mandy Dees & Pam Colley 2005*

(1950s) Tiny room, seating was a wooden bench around the walls. He did not have a receptionist, so when you entered you looked round to see who was before you. Large bottles of medicines were placed on shelves above.

*Margaret Biggs 2005*

Clinic in Memorial Hall c.1950 with Dr Godfrey & Mrs Malkin          *P Leyman*

An Infant Welfare clinic was set up in the Memorial Hall in 1951 by Dr Malkin's wife Gwendoline to take pressure off the surgery.
    * issue dried milk, orange juice and Virol.
    * set of scales
    * pamphlets on babies food
    * advice on spots and pimples
    * cup of tea and biscuits
    * toys for the toddlers
*volunteers brought mothers and babies in by car from outlying areas*

*from WI history 1977*

Godfrey Malkin retired to South Devon in 1965, and was succeeded by Patrick Ramage who had joined him in 1963. Patrick and Mary Ramage took over the surgery and home at Mona –

Dr Malkin retires 1965

P Leyman

*"What brought you to Fownhope?"* Pure accident. We came through Prof Harding Raynes who had a weekend cottage at Lea Brink who asked me to help Dr Malkin out because he was finding it difficult to cope on his own. I just came to see what country general practice was like. We had a look at the practice and the area, liked it and decided to come.

The surgery was antiquated and small. You had to erect a couch in the surgery to examine a patient and then fold it up. You did all your own dispensing, answered the phone, wrote your own letters. Surgery started by 9am and finish at 12 or 1 o'clock. Patients didn't have transport, visits were normal, then we started evening surgery about 5.30pm. It usually went on until the pubs closed, about 10.30pm. There were no appointments. There were probably around 1800 patients scattered around Fownhope.

The most I ever had was 29 visits in one day in February in 1966 or 1967 when the weather stopped people getting down, and there was a lot of illness, flu and chesty problems. I went out in all weather day and night and weekends. The only time I couldn't was in very heavy snow in 1982 when the snow must have been at least 15feet high, but I got through to most places except Checkley. I went over to a four wheel drive Range Rover in the 1970s. We had the dispensary and drugs put on our first computer in 1982 so we could print prescriptions. We could check with batch numbers what you'd given someone. We could order our drugs from the wholesalers. Then we put a patient register on the computer.

Dr Patrick Ramage talking to David & Margaret Clark, 2005

Patrick's patients were titled people, landed gentry, professionals, farm and country workers and local people and gypsies who couldn't read and write. He had patients to the edge of Hereford and Ross, Ballingham, Little Dewchurch and Woolhope.

*Mary Ramage with Pam Colley & Margaret Clark, 2006*

| DR PATRICK RAMAGE Surgery consulting hours 1978 | | | | |
|---|---|---|---|---|
| *Monday* | *Tuesday* | *Wednesday* | *Thursday* | *Friday* |
| 9-10 | 9-10 | 9-10 | 9-10 | 9-10 |
| 6-7pm | | 6-7pm | | 6-7pm |

Dr Ramage 1968          *N Cope*    The Rowans & church spire    *D M Clark*

Patrick Ramage set out his services in a leaflet in 1990. There were surgeries by appointment six mornings, and three evenings each week. Patients were encouraged to attend surgery but could also have a home visit. Patrick Ramage and Dr Jonathan Ingham at Tarrington, provided emergency cover between them. The Health Care team included Mary Ramage as full-time Practice Manager with six part-time staff to handle reception and dispensing duties, plus a nurse, Gillian Stoakes, health visitor, Edith Stevenson, and the attached District Nurse. Clinics included advice on smoking etc, Asthma, Diabetes, Family Planning and Well Baby, with annual checks for those aged over 75.

### District Nurse
#### Pat Homan worked along side
"Came to live in Fownhope (*Scotch Firs*) in 1968, but provided cover for Fownhope from Stoke Edith since 1960. I was midwife, general district nurse, health visitor and school nurse as well, covering Fownhope, Mordiford and Woolhope. I also had to relieve the nurses who lived in Little Birch and Withington. People contacted me by phone early in the morning, or else I was out until lunch-time. I left a slate in the window to say I'll be visiting such a place, and they could follow me round if urgent. I got one day off a week, one weekend a month, otherwise I was on call."

*Pat Homan talking to Janet Jones & Mandy Dees Aug 2005*

**12** THE HEREFORD TIMES, THURSDAY, JULY 16, 1992

# Row over surgery causes village split

A BID to build a new surgery to improve care for the community has split a Herefordshire village.

Highway chiefs say visibility at the access to the site at Fownhope is "critically substandard" and development would "exacerbate an already hazardous situation".

Now councillors are to see for themselves whether the position of the scheme is acceptable.

Dr Patrick Ramage hopes to build a new surgery and take in another partner to

parking space on an unclassified road next to Bowen's Farm to replace premises which were built more than 25 years ago.

He said the present buildings were short of space and are totally inadequate for current medical needs.

No other site within the village boundary could have been developed to provide adequate medical services or provide for further changes in future requirements.

Dr Ramage also hoped to

improve care.

Herefordshire Community Health Council has supported the new surgery. It said the practice list was increasing, while physical accommodation for patients failed to meet modern standards.

Athough the site is outside development limits, South Herefordshire planning officers thought it was acceptable in principle, given the limited potential for development in Fownhope.

The plans have prompted at least 37 letters supporting

the proposal to be sent to the district council and 24 letters of objection, while a show of hands at a parish council meeting found 104 people in favour and only eight against.

The county highway authority recommended the plan be rejected due to poor visibility and the increased traffic on a substandard-width road.

A panel of South Herefordshire councillors agreed to visit the site before making a decision on the plans.

### New Medical Centre 1992-4
Patrick Ramage was ill in 1987 and considered early retirement. The *Health Authority* did not want to see another single-handed practice. Fownhope could have lost its doctor *(as Tarrington did)*. Patrick opted to expand the service and find new premises. He and Mary looked for ideas from Sussex to Scotland. They looked at Ringfield House but the conversion costs were high. Planning permission was obtained for a new surgery next to Bowens Farm but the farmer then raised the price of the land. Patrick found another site – an acre of Island Orchard *(owned in the 18th century by another notable doctor, Thomas Paytherus!)* – which got the blessing of a village meeting *(104 votes to 8)*, and planning consent in 1992. The new building cost £350,000, opened in 1994, to house three GPs, and serve 20 surrounding villages.

**Christopher Allen** had joined the practice in 1990, and developed the medical centre with two more partners, a range of nursing colleagues and a well-equipped dispensary.to serve 4,500 patients. He lives across the river at Carey. He took on Brockhampton Court in 1996 and converted the former hotel into a 48 bed nursing and care complex.

Opening new centre          *S Clifford*

Medical Centre 2005     *D M Clark*

| Fownhope Surgery consulting hours Sept 2004 | | | | |
| --- | --- | --- | --- | --- |
| *Monday* | *Tuesday* | *Wednesday* | *Thursday* | *Friday* |
| 8.30-11.00 | 8.30-11.00 | 8.30-11.00 | 8.30-11.00 | 8.30-11.00 |
| 4-6pm | 4-6pm | 4-6pm | | 4-6pm |
| *Dispensary* | | | | |
| 9-1pm | 9-1pm | 9-1pm | 9-2.30pm | 9-1pm |
| 2.30-6.30pm | 2.30-6.30pm | 2.30-6.30pm | closed | 2.30-6.30pm |

## WRVS MEALS on WHEELS

The WRVS volunteers service was well-established before 1970, described here by Rachael Best:

"I became WRVS Area Organiser for meals on wheels in 1970, taking over from Mrs Judy Mills. Fownhope covers from Dormington and Hampton Bishop to Sollers Hope. We have always delivered two meals a week and in the 1970s the journey would cover 50 miles. Taking meals to remote farm cottages where we would have to walk across fields to deliver. Meals were collected from kitchens in Hereford, put in a round metal container with lids. A typical meal was meat and two vegetables, with pudding. Gravy and custard were served from thermos flasks. The meal tins were stacked in charcoal heated containers in the boot of the car. 26-30 meals were delivered per day at a cost of 5d a meal."

### WRVS VOLUNTEERS 1970-2006

| | | | |
|---|---|---|---|
| Shirley Allan * | Madge Daines | Margaret Jolley | Judy Sharman |
| Tom Austin | Gaynor Furse | Ann Jordan | Derek Smith |
| Constance Austin | Joan Flint | Ann Keeling | Margaret Skelton |
| Betty Barnett * | Mrs Fensome | Bill Lewis | Peggy Twidale |
| Mrs Bristow | Mandy Gunn | Margaret Mais | Shirley Taylor |
| Michael Best | Joan Garnett | Margaret Mason | Enid Turner |
| Philippa Banks | Margaret Garnett | Judy Mills | Rene Thomas * |
| Mrs Frank Brock | Julie Goodwin | Beryl Moss * | Sue Tetlow |
| Rachael Best ** | Joan Hambleton * | Gladys Newman * | Kath Watkins |
| Brenda Coleman * | Penny Hall | Beverly Platford * | Sue Watkins |
| Jan Canavan | Joan Hill | Mary Palmer | Pippa Wheeler |
| Mrs Cassidy | Marie Hammonds * | Edith Perkins | Rosemary Whitmey |
| Muriel Cornish | Joy Hayward | Elizabeth Rimmer | |
| Joan Davies * | Irene Holman | Pat Sullivan * | *List Compiled By* |
| Pat Dickerson | Averil Jones | George Sharman | *Rachael Best* |

*\* 10 yrs long service certificate (10)*      *\*\* 25yrs long service medal & bar (1)*

Joan Davies delivering Christmas meal/gift to Dickie Brookes
at The Folly, Common Hill from Rachael Best's 1965 Morris Minor

We often had great concern for our 'clients' as heating, lighting and hot water supplies were basic or non-existent. However they had been through two world wars and were very resilient. With Faulkner House being built in 1972 a number of 'clients' moved into this warm and safe environment, no longer needing meals on wheels.

## and Meals On Wheels 2006

"Now in 2006 we deliver 8-10 meals with a journey of 32 miles. Each meal costs £2.35p, collected from new WRVS kitchens in Hereford.

Pre-frozen meals are prepared in special ovens for delivery within one and a half hours. My task as organiser has been made so easy by the able assistance of volunteer helpers. I have had little difficulty in finding new volunteers. My job is to arrange for meals for new clients, assess their dietary needs, and prepare a quarterly roster for teams of driver and assistant, each delivering once per month. Special contingencies are made for four wheel vehicles in snow or extreme flood conditions."

# THE SCHOOL

| School's Headteachers | | | |
|---|---|---|---|
| *1893* | * Joseph Booth Marshall | *1977* | Eric A Solesbury |
| *1923* | * Henry A Procter | *1994* | Martin Chapple |
| *1943* | * Miss R M Owens, later Davies | *1998* | Colin Mutton |
| *1944* | * Mrs Eleanor Pugh | *2003* | Allyson Taylor |
| *1960* | * Henry W Pain | * | *resident* |

Joseph Booth Marshall held the fort for some thirty years. He had a fine reputation and played an active part in the community, most notably as secretary of the celebrated *Flower Festival* in the pre-war years. By 1919 he seems to have found discipline difficult, and must have been glad to retire in 1923.

"Mr Marshall was a good but strict teacher. His cane was always to hand and we were in disgrace, both at school and home, if it had been used on us. Mr Marshall suffered with gout in his feet and this made him rather short tempered at times; his affliction did not deter his presence as he rarely had time off."

*Helena Rose Biggs née Watkins school before the war*

School 1929 

*J Hardwick*

## *Harry Procter 1923-43*

Harry Procter, came from Derby, and lived in the school house with his wife Lottie who taught sewing and crafts. Procter was also church organist and choir master, and occasionally had to miss school to perform at funeral services. Numbers on the school roll ranged from 52 to 75. The school had two or three classes. Procter always taught the seniors, other teachers included Mrs Avery for 16 years, and Mrs Averill who taught here for 7 years. *Midland Red's* bus service, extended in 1926, brought student teachers from Hereford Training College on teaching practice. Miss Owens (one of the students) must have been impressed – she returned in 1942 as headteacher.

---

**INSPECTOR'S REPORT 1926**

'The HEADMASTER, is EARNEST and thoughtful, has secured children's willing co-operation. In his class reading is fluent, prose extracts recited with expression … arithmetic is neat', Oral questioning on work in History & Geography elicited a very poor response. The boys are more alert at Physical Exercises than the girls. The infants talk freely about the interesting pictures which have been collected.

---

School 1935 with Harry Procter

*School*

The School catered for children from 5 to 14, though some children left at 11 with scholarships to Hereford High School. Getting children to come to school had been an uphill battle in the late 19th century. In Procter's day it was easier with regular home visits by the attendance officer. Attendances rose from 72% when Procter first arrived to around 87% ten years later. There were incentives – when the attendance reached an average of more than 93% the whole school was awarded an extra days holiday!

The school year started after Easter, with a week or fortnight for Whitsun, six weeks for hop-picking from mid August to early October, and two weeks at Christmas. There were extra days for the Church Choir's outing, the Friday before the Club walk and the Flower Show, and polling day at election times. School was closed by epidemics and by bad weather – the area was snowbound for a week three winters in a row in the 1940s.

Old school                    *P Leyman*

School reunion 1988           *D Biggs*

The core subjects were reading, writing, arithmetic and scripture with some time for drawing and nature study, and history and geography for older pupils. Mrs Procter taught crafts – the girls learnt sewing, darning and needlework – the boys basketry, weaving and book crafts. The boys also looked after plots in the school garden. The village WI hosted an exhibition of school craft in 1936, displayed at the annual *Arts and Crafts Society* in Hereford Town Hall in 1936 and again in 1938. Sales of work in the Memorial Hall produced enough in 1938 to buy a new sewing machine, and pay for the school's Christmas party!

The seniors' syllabus was very much directed to the world of work. Short courses in dairying were held in the Memorial Hall in alternate years from 1937 with a four week course on cookery and domestic science in other years for which an electric cooker was temporarily installed. Girls only you might think, but you'd be wrong – boys also attended without any signs of fuss. Some produce was sold at the end of the course.

"One of our teachers walked with us to school daily, past Hardwick's farm until we and the Halford girls were a bit older.
On my way home from school I would stop and talk to an itinerant stone-breaker and watch him at work. In those days it seemed safe to wander about and talk to strangers and I never heard of harm coming to anyone."
*Tom Plumley, nephew of Harry Procter, school 1929 to 1938, lived at Irongate on Capler Lane*

The school's wireless introduced in 1929 provided a string of lessons on the wider world outside – from slate quarrying in north Wales to life in distant Burma. It seems that only the senior boys got to these sessions – the senior girls did sewing with Mrs Procter.

The vicar took scripture once week and made other visits as a school manager (governor) as did other managers, notably Mrs Mabel Fox JP, who took a keen interest in needlework. The whole school went to church on Ascension Day, Ash Wednesday and Armistice Day.

Fownhope's school building was 60 years old when Procter became head. It was difficult to keep warm – on cold days children had to huddle round the fire – it was too cold to do any written work. Henry Procter suffered from lumbago and phlebitis so he must have dreaded those days. The playground was fenced in 1925, and given a tarmac surface in 1938. It was quite an event when the county council provided new desks and tables in 1939.

"Uncle Harry kept what would today be considered strict control in class, my brother and I were rightly shown no favours. But off-parade was a different matter. I have him to thank for taking me to St. Andrews where I saw the Birmingham City and England goalkeeper Harry Hibbs play – the greatest of thrills for a young captain of the school team. He also took me to Worcester where I saw the great Don Bradman score a century. Childless themselves, they liked me to accompany them on trips to Ross although I was never sure which one of us was looking after the other! Aunt Lottie would take me on train journeys to Monmouth and picnics on the Malvern Hills. The sun always shone on those days."
*nephew Tom Plumley*

Epidemics were a sad feature of school and village life – smallpox, mumps, chicken pox, whooping cough, ringworm, measles, impetigo and pink-eye are all recorded in the logs – the school had to close for 3 weeks when scarlet fever hit the village in 1934. There were regular visits by nurse Andrews, and the dentist, with dental treatment on the school premises! Godfrey Malkin, the new village doctor inoculated pupils against diphtheria in 1941.

There were no school meals when Henry Procter took over. Miss Nott, the vicar's daughter, gave cocoa and oxo as refreshments from 1926. Horlicks was introduced in 1935 when 38 of the children bought a third of a pint of the malt beverage for a half penny a time. By 1941 that it had been replaced at the same price by milk from the *Marketing Board*. School dinners were provided for 23 of the 57 children by June 1943.

The whole school closed for the annual choir trip which took children by charabanc to Malvern, Tewkesbury and Cheltenham (all in one day in 1927), and to Stratford, Porthcawl, Mumbles and Weston-Super-Mare in other years.

The senior boys football team kicked off in 1936 with games against four rival schools – Woolhope, Brockhampton, How Caple and Mordiford. The vicar, Rev Charles Cottrell took the boys to one of their first games at Mordiford – two in his car, while the other nine cycled there and back. We dont know the results! Whiterdine field was used for school cricket in June 1939.

Lower school 1947          *Joyce Davies*   Upper school 1947          *Joyce Davies*

Sports day was a big event – held each August from 1927 by courtesy of Mr Greenow in Whiterdine field with events for pupils and old boys and girls too.

## School Sports August 1927

Among those present were the Vicar, Misses Nott, Dr and Mrs Baggs, Mr Leslie Tompson, the Misses McPhee, and a large number of parents and friends The judges were Mr Bayliss, Mr Robbins and Mr Leslie Tompson. Mr Procter acted as handicapper. Every child who failed to win a prize in the sports was awarded a small gift of money in consolation. Tom Biggs made a speech on behalf of his fellow scholars thanking Mr and Mrs Procter (and) Mr Greenow for the loan of the field for the sports.

The winners were:

Infants' race   1. Ernest Godsell   2. Edna Reed   3. Alice Bennett

100 yards, boys over 11:

1. Tom Biggs   2. Edgar Painter   3. Edwin Godsell

100 yards girls over 11

1. Alice Biggs;   2. Florence Godsell;   3. Eileen Bennett

80 yards boys under 11

1. Fred Smith   2. Dick Welling   3. Harry Mace

80 yards girls under 11

1. Margery Davies;   2. Mary Reed;   3. Vera Biggs

Egg and spoon race girls

1. Alice Biggs   2. Barbara Godsell   3. Olive Painter

Three-legged race

1. Edgar Painter and Arthur Davies;   2. Florence Godsell and Vera Biggs
3. Tom Lowe and Jim Flower

440 yards boys   1. Tom Biggs   2. Tom Lowe   3. Arthur Davies

Consolation race boys

1. Sidney Harper;   2. Edwin Jones   3. David Biggs

girls   1. Iris Sloman;   2. Madge Smith   3. Madeline Hardwick

Old girls race, 100 yards:

1. Mrs Mace;   2. Miss May Flower   3. Miss Betty Biggs

Old boys 220 yards   1. Jim Grundy;   2. Ivor Haines   3. W. Tyler

*Hereford Times*

The Christmas party brought presents of sweets, fruit and books from school managers and from Harry Lloyd the shopkeeper at West End Stores. There was a gramophone in 1925. In the 1920s the school celebrated egg day before Easter – eggs were taken to the children's ward at Hereford Hospital.

When the Procters retired in October 1942 there was a large farewell from managers and parents who raised the princely sum of £26 14 shillings to celebrate their contribution to the school, the church and village life. £26 may not sound much – but its the equivalent of about £2,900 in 2005 terms – a remarkably generous amount for cash-strapped war-time Fownhope.

## The War Years

Henry Procter was succeeded by Miss RM Owen who took a week's leave to get married, returned as Mrs Davies, and soon moved on to be replaced by Mrs Eleanor Pugh in 1944 who served as head for the next 15 years.

Few other teachers stayed long. The exception, Frances Daffin, later Mrs Charles, stayed three years. One unqualified teacher Mrs Wade lasted only a month. She went missing in January 1945 – a fortnight later the head received a message to say she was *"considered left school"*.

The School played an important part in the war effort. Older boys were allowed to work on the land and holidays were extended to give time for the autumn harvest. The whole school had two or three weeks extra holiday each July to work on the fruit harvest and hay-making. Some boys were given time off to join in the potato harvest. The senior children also attended a dairying course held in the Memorial Hall.

Fownhope's *Home Guard*, formed in 1939, left no records. The school prepared for air raids, with visits by the air wardens to learn to handle respirators and gas masks. The School closed for a few days in July 1940 so that the school windows could be made safer against the impact of bomb blast. Fortunately this was never tested.

Many activities closed for the war. There was no choir outing, sports day, flower show or club walk. *Midland Red's* bus service was halved to conserve petrol though some student teachers managed to travel in from Hereford College. However the boy's football team continued while Charles Cottrell was vicar.

Children and families were moved from those areas most at risk from *luftwaffe* bombing. There were 17 evacuees out of a roll of 68 by December 1940 – a quarter of all pupils. Some didn't settle to village life – two children returned to Bristol in the following May, and several more returned to the London area in 1942, though there was a further wave of evacuees when the *Nazi* assault reached its second peak in summer of 1944 – the logbook records seven new evacuee pupils out of a roll of 52.

The School's reputation for handicrafts under Lottie Procter was put to very good use. Pupils were busy knitting mittens, blankets and scarves which were sent to three 'old boys' serving in France in 1940, merchant seamen, evacuees from occupied Finland and the local Home Guard and WVS. Boys repaired books for children at Poulstone hostel at Kings Caple and patients in the Red Cross hospital. Toys and scarves were sent to the school set up by Mrs JB Priestley (wife of the famous writer) at Titley Court near Kington.

The school's *National Savings Group* collected some £14 by October 1941- the equivalent of £1,400 in today's earnings. The Rural Pennies Fund encouraged children to give a penny a week to the Red Cross war effort. Money was sent to St Dunstans hospital for men blinded in the war. Children even collected money for the *Overseas Tobacco Fund* – presumably buying cigarettes for servicemen.

The introduction of all-year summertime in November 1940 meant that the school day started at 9.30 and closed at 3.45pm. The school was a cold place in the harsh winters of the early 1940s. *"Children are unable to get rid of their colds because of the cold school. They sit and shiver"*. The temperature never exceeded 52° F (11°C) in one three week period. Coal was in short supply and there were many power cuts – one WI meeting in the adjacent Memorial Hall had to get by on two candles! A new stove, installed in the School in December 1944 was very welcome.

Fownhope School had more than its fair share of epidemics during the cold bleak war years which kept many from school. There were two epidemics of German measles, followed by mumps and later by whooping cough in December 1943 when the attendance fell to 40% before the school had to be closed.

School dinners, started in June 1943, proved popular with 23 of the 57 children sitting down for the meal. Mrs Biggs of Canon House, wife of the long-serving school manager and churchwarden, kept the books as school 'treasurer'.

Eleanor Pugh must have been relieved when war ended in May 1945 – her entry in the LogBook however seems slightly subdued – *"Today is V.E. Day. The flag was flown this morning and the children had a little celebration."* They certainly deserved it.

The post war years brought fresh challenges for Eleanor Pugh – adverse weather, closure threats and accommodating older pupils from the surrounding area.

Tower 1952                                                      *School*

## The Senior Centre 1948-58

The school-leaving age was raised from 14 to 15. Herefordshire Council had to provide secondary modern schools for those not selected for grammar school places. There was no money to pay for new school buildings. Ideas for new infants and junior schools at Mordiford to serve surrounding villages, including Fownhope, came to nothing. Instead the county tried to meet the spirit of the Butler Act by creating a new senior class to serve the schools in the area. Fownhope was chosen. It was the biggest of the four local schools, and Eleanor Pugh was an experienced head.

Science 1952                                                    *School*

Fownhope's senior centre came into being in January 1948 catering for 13 to 15 year olds drawn from four schools – Mordiford, Woolhope, Holme Lacy and Fownhope. There were 22 in the senior class under Charles Jacob. The Butler Act had specified that secondary education should be for all those over the age of 11, but here the 12 year olds remained in the top junior class with Mrs Pugh in the existing school building. So the senior centre had just one teacher to look after children from three different year groups. It must have been pretty daunting to try to teach such a wide range in just one class. By 1949 arrangements had been made to bus scholars to Tupsley once a week where the boys did woodwork and the girls did house-craft with children from other all-age schools.

The senior centre moved in to a HORSA hut on the school playground. Mrs Pugh noted in the school log-book that it took time for children from different villages to settle down together – she had to punish two boys for persistent trouble. The school inspectors made frequent visits. Their solution was to add the 12 year olds to the senior class, boosting numbers from 22 to 28 by September 1951.

Gardening 1952                    *School*  Music 1952                    *School*

Charles Jacob had a hard time but made progress. The inspectors were impressed by basketry work in the senior centre. Pupils found out more about the rocks of the Fownhope area, and made a model of the Woolhope Dome which was displayed at the *Three Counties* show. It must have looked good because Mr Jacob made a return trip to the Show in June 1953 to display the work of the Fownhope seniors, though he emigrated to Canada a month later!

He was replaced by Donald W Richardson from Stretton Sugwas. By now all the senior children from Woolhope had joined the school but there were still only 27 pupils in the senior centre. Mr Richardson made a feature of physical training – the school competed in the Hereford and District Sports, got to play football matches, beating near rivals Much Marcle by some 11 goals to one in the Herefordshire rural schools cup, before being knocked out by Puddleston Court 2-0. And the senior centre gave Fownhope children some glimpses into the outside world. Mr Richardson took them on a trip to Hereford waterworks, followed by a day out at Dudley Zoo. Nothing quite like that had happened in the pre-war years.

But the senior centre was a far cry from the ideals of the 1944 Act. The centre might have been viable if there had been the space to house four classes, one for each year group. The diocesan surveyor looked at ways to extend the HORSA hut to create more space. But numbers were too low, and weren't helped by the school's success in getting more pupils into grammar schools and Hereford Technical College. So by 1958 the county and the diocese decided that Fownhope's 40 seniors should join the new Bishop's school at Tupsley.

The change must have come as a real shock to the Fownhope children who had previously spent their entire schooling days in the cosy surroundings of their home village. Now they had to adjust to the rigours of the bus trip. No longer 28 children in one class straddling three age groups. Now Fownhope children had to cope in a large school with many pupils coming not only from 'strange' villages but from the city too. Fownhope school roll dropped from over 100 to just 56 but the school survived. And that 'temporary' HORSA hut? It became home for the school's infant class.

Woolhope School closed in July 1959, and its 17 pupils were bussed to Fownhope to use the surplus space. Brockhampton survived till it too was closed in 1976 – and pupils travelled by mini-bus to Fownhope, joined by their teacher, Mrs Farrington, and the school's grand piano!

### Closure 1951?

In the meantime the school itself had survived a plan in 1951 to amalgamate smaller rural schools.

"Proposed that Fownhope should lose its school and the children ... transported to Mordiford ... which had better facilities for enlargement, and for games. On the other hand Fownhope was already a much larger village and likely to increase considerably ... managers consulted the PTA ... some parents regarded the fact that Mordiford could supply a football field as being much the most important element the LEA decided that a temporary extra class room should be built at Fownhope ... Fownhope School was saved."

*Wilf Chignell, chairman 1951*

One teacher who really made a difference was **Mary Soulsby**, a Tynesider, who came to Whiterdine Place opposite School in 1951 with her architect husband John. Both played an important part in village life for half a century. She was class and supply teacher for many years, a leading member of WI, key player in the two WI histories in 1955 and 1977, church-goer and chorister, noted artist, guider and member of village orchestra. Eleanor Pugh praised her publicly in 1954 –

"Has given excellent service. Her class management has made a great difference in the 'tone' of the younger children."

### Henry Pain 1960-1977

Henry Pain was the last head to live in the School House. He was in post for 17 years with his wife Mary as deputy for some of that time. During this time the school ventured on trips to London, Cardiff and Bristol, went swimming at Mordiford, and bought a tape recorder. The school attracted some media attention in 1972 when a newly appointed teacher, Judith Pumphrey, was murdered at Bridstow.

Class in 1974                                                                 *School*

The 1868 school was a fine building but difficult to heat. In the winter of 1963 the thermometer dropped to 28°F (-2°C) in the Infants classroom. The school was closed for a week.

The chimney was condemned, part of the ceiling fell in in 1969 and again in 1974, and there were serious water shortages. Numbers fell to just 54 pupils in 1968, but the arrival of mains water unleashed an era of rapid house-building which almost trebled the school roll to 133 pupils in 1975.

When the Pains retired in 1977 the school went to church for a presentation by the Vicar of a silver candelabra and bone china tea service, gifts of the whole village as a token of affection

*"Today I Henry W. Pain and my wife Mary M. J. Pain resign our respective positions as Head and Deputy Head of Fownhope School. There have been many changes during our seventeen years seven months at the school, and we hope we leave it somewhat better than it was when we took over in Jan 1960."*

Hockey with Rev Sell          *P Leyman*   Class 1976                    *School*

## A New School 1979

The Rural District Council agreed in 1967 to buy 7 acres of Church Croft for housing and a new school (two acres, cost £2,200) with a shared playing field. A temporary classroom was erected to the rear of the Memorial Hall in 1971. The school managers, led by Margaret Biggs, Joe Chamberlain, Gina Children and Ray Howard Jones wanted a new building. Nigel Dees, a descendant of the Stones who had helped build the old school, designed a £130,000 building which was twice the limit imposed by the government spending cap. So the managers persuaded the new county council in 1975 to fund the first phase with extra classrooms and a kitchen on the new site, and then came back for a second bite to complete the job in February 1978. The old HORSA hut was demolished in September 1978. By January 1979 the whole school was under one roof. It was a remarkably achievement.

The old school building found new life. The Parish Council leased it from the Diocese in 1979 for 'community use', including squash courts until the new Memorial Hall was opened in October 1987.

New school 2006                                                    *A Corby*

### Eric Solesbury 1977-94

Eric Solesbury served as head for served 17 years, with a staff of five teachers, with 125 children on the school roll in 1983. His life was so very different from earlier heads – a diary filled with 'heads' conferences, 'pyramid' meetings, staff training courses, and the new world of SATs, Key Stages, local management, computers, governor sub-committees and information sheets for parents. Fortunately Eric maintained a range of school sports – football, netball and rounders, as well as music and drama. There was a choir, recorder group, French club, photography club, and visits to Malvern theatre. Eighteen pupils went to the Hereford music festival in 1987. Lilian Thomas and Jane Taylor took on school meals as volunteers when the county service ceased in 1982, producing 80 meals in the school kitchens – roast chicken, veg and gravy for 45p each – with apple crumble for another 10p! Mrs Farrington who had come to teach at the school when Brockhampton closed, stayed until 1985.

The School has had three heads since Eric Solesbury and has managed to keep a roll of around 100 pupils, albeit with resources that earlier heads could only dream of!

Leavers 1990                                                    *Jane Davies*

Leavers 1990 with Mr Solesbury                                 *Jane Davies*

# School Budgets Then and Now

Fownhope School's budget was £295,000 for the year 2005-6, compared with just over £159 in 1898-99.

£159 in 1898 is worth about £63,000 at today's earnings, or £107,000 on the basis of the country's wealth.

| | 1898-99 | | 2005-6 |
|---|---|---|---|
| | actual £ | *at 2005's wealth £* | £ |
| Teachers' salaries | 115 | *76,961* | 239,734 |
| Cleaning & maintenance | 4.33 | *3,976* | 9,000 |
| Water & sewerage | nil | *nil* | 820 |
| Energy | 8.48 | *5,822* | 5,000 |
| Rates | 1 | *669* | 1,000 |
| Stationery equipment etc | 12.61 | *8,439* | 19,952 |
| Insurance | 0.52 | *351* | 767 |
| New building work | 16 | *10,708* | 5,720 |
| Total | 159.51 | *106,748* | 295,883 |
| *Pupils* | *112* | | *100* |

Leavers 1997      *Jane Davies*

# LIBRARIES and MEDIA

Fownhope's first library had been set up in 1900 in the doctor's house at Highland Place opposite the Church by Mrs Anna Jones, with some 100 books.

Highland Place 2006                                              *A Corby*

The County Council set up a part-time 'deposit' library in 1926 in the School with the head as librarian. It was one more chore for the hard-pressed head which Eleanor Pugh does not seem to have enjoyed. The library was open for two brief sessions each week after school with 3 shelves containing 250 books. The library van changed the stock three times a year. There were only 25 adult readers in 1952 – more used the Hereford libraries. It was well used by scholars – *'most girls read, but not all boys'*.

The private library ceased in 1952 and the stock of books was sold off. The adult library in the School stopped in 1956 when the county librarian included Fownhope in monthly schedule for the travelling library, with brief calls each month in different parts of the parish.

The Parish Council was not impressed and campaigned for a permanent library building and suggested sites in Court Orchard or the New Inn in 1956. The Parish widened this to library and resource centre with support from a parish poll in 1999.

The mobile library changed several times in the 1990s and underwent further changes in July 2007 when new schedules provided brief weekly calls at the Church, Scotch Firs and the Green Man with a home delivery service for house-bound readers.

| Mobile Library calls 2005- second Monday each month | | | |
|---|---|---|---|
| Old Lodge | 9.20-30 | Court Drive | 11.00-15 |
| Rowans Capler Lane | 9.35-45 | Court Orchard | 11.20-35 |
| Church | 9.50-10.15 | Noverwood Drive | 11.40-50 |
| Scotch Firs | 10.20-55 | Common Hill | 11.55-12.20 |

**RIDGE HILL MAST**
mast 160metres high, weighs about 200 tons
*transmits radio & TV to 500,000 people in 3 counties*
first television VHF signals in 1968, UHF in 1972

Mobile library                    *S Gough*

## Parish Magazines

There is no record of any early parish magazine though Woolhope's dates back to the 1890s. Local news coverage relied on the Hereford newspapers, and on brief entries in the church deanery news from the late 1920s. Wilf Chignell edited the first monthly parish magazine in 1950, *Triple Parish News*, which provided a wide range of news, events and local adverts for Fownhope, Brockhampton, Woolhope and Mordiford. Vera E Biggs organised the production for ten years from 1950. It ceased about 1965 when his successor, Claude Sell, could not find a volunteer editor, but was revived in 1974 by Ray Howard Jones, covering Hampton Bishop too, and has continued as *The Beneficial* covering church news for the united parish. *Contact*, a 2 page bi-monthly listing, published by the Parochial Church Council, was started in 1968, edited first by Derrick Brown, and later by Margaret Skelton. *The Flag* began in 1996, edited by Ann Corby to provide more space for news and comment, supported by adverts and a parish council grant, and distributed monthly to every household in the parish.

## Television

Television was a novelty until the 1960s. Harry Fagg, publican at the *Green Man*, was a fan, but had to admit that the quality of the reception in 1949 from the Sutton Coldfield transmitter was pretty poor. Fownhope made the screen when the village orchestra performed in an early broadcast from Birmingham in 1952. Reception improved with the opening of the Ridge Hill transmitter on Marcle Ridge which beamed VHF signals to the village in 1968.

# CHURCH and CHAPELS

The Church and chapels played a key part in the community in 1919. There was a resident vicar and a curate to serve Fownhope and Brockhampton. The School's head was also church organist and choirmaster. Half the adult population were on the Church electoral roll in the period between 1941 *(225 out of 448)* and 1961. Numbers fell to 124 in 1991 despite the increase in population but the Church remains a major force in the community.

Church watercolour – some artistic licence        *J Soulsby*

"We were brought up a fairly strict Christian family. On Sunday only essential work was done on the farm, such as milking, watering and feeding the animals and birds. We children were not allowed to play card games. We all went to Church for 11a.m service. We, the children, went to Sunday School at 2.30pm and all of us went again to Evensong."

*Lionel Biggs born 1925, brought up at Lechmere Ley*

## The Clergy

Fownhope's Vicars served the parish of Fownhope including Fawley, as well as Brockhampton. Since 1994 the four parishes of Fownhope, Brockhampton, Woolhope and Mordiford have come together in a joint benefice – with churchwardens and Parochial Church Councils for each parish. The incumbent now carries the title of Rector.

119

Church 1913     *S Clifford*     Church inside     *B Snape*

Frederick Nott served for some 32 years, but his four successors only stayed 19 years between them. Edward Weeden had been a curate in East London and Bombay. Gerald Bourdillon, a Cambridge graduate, moved to Pembridge in 1937, but his wife came back for the church fete in 1940:

---

Come and enjoy yourselves! Grand Fete in aid of ambulance scheme
Church Croft Fownhope, today, Saturday 29 June. Opening ceremony at 3.15 p.m. by Mrs. Bourdillon. Fancy Dress Parade ( money prizes) Competitions, side shows, children's sports Admission 6d

*Hereford Times, June 1940*

---

Charles Cottrell played an active part in school life but shared his parish duties with that of army chaplain. Edwin Preston, who had a 'first' in chemistry and a masters degree from Liverpool, taught during the week. He went back to full-time teaching in 1947, but returned as vicar of Woolhope in 1966.

120

Preston, with some help from Father Oman, an unpaid curate, conducted 5 or 6 services each Sunday in 1944

| Fownhope | Brockhampton | Fawley |
|---|---|---|
| 8, 11, and 6.30 pm | 3.30 | 2.30 |

Rev Cottrell 1940    *P Leyman*

Welcome home 1945    *J Newman*

Wilf Chignell was only here 8 years but made a real impact on the Church and on the life of the community. He served on the parish and district councils, saw off the school closure threat as chairman of the governors, mapped out the local footpaths, set up the parish magazine and the youth club and revived the Scouts. The village orchestra was his brainchild. He found time to play cricket at Brockhampton, and wrote a history of the Worcestershire club.

Claude Sell must have found it hard to follow Chiggie. Claude clocked up 121 hospital visits in 1959, and spent £107 on postage, phone and car mileage. He was well-regarded by the Darby and Joans club, the Young Wives, and the school footballers who presented him with gifts when he left in 1970 to go to Weobley. Ray Howard Jones evoked similar affection to Chiggie. He helped revive the youth club and parish magazine and was a force in the battle to persuade a reluctant education authority that Fownhope needed a new school building. He was also the Bishop's communications adviser and broadcast on local radio. Attendances at church services increased in his early years from 5059 in 1972 to 6469 in 1974. He and his wife Jill were the first incumbents to live in the new vicarage, built in the grounds of the old vicarage.

Lychgate opening ceremony 1953

*P Leyman*

Jill Howard Jones combined her 16 years at the vicarage with teaching in Hereford and writing – here she captured the spirit of Christmas at the new Vicarage:

Sixteen Christmases at Fownhope Vicarage have rolled into one. They seem captured in a magic time warp.

During the Christmas period, the doorbell would ring constantly. Frequently there was nobody there. Instead, a present would be left on the step – sacks of potatoes, baskets of apples, bottles of sherry, even a duck prepared for the oven.

The church is floodlight; mumbling shadows bunch at the lych-gate; the village gathers for the service. Inside there is that special hushed expectation peculiar to the Midnight Mass. Proud parents smile over the heads of offspring home for Christmas. The organ plays. The service is about to begin. At last Christmas is here.

*from 'A Herefordshire Christmas', compiled by D Green, pub Alan Sutton 1993*

Rev Sell                                    *P Leyman*   R Howard Jones 1980  *P Leyman*

Anthony Dixon became Rector of Fownhope when the united benefice was formed in 1994. His successor Will Pridie has a very different Sunday schedule from that of the 1940s, only made possible with help from retired clergy and lay readers such as Christopher Whitmey and Dennis Evans:

| Fownhope | Mordiford | Brockhampton | Woolhope | Checkley |
|----------|-----------|--------------|----------|----------|
| 11.00    | 9.45      | 8.30         | 11.00    | 9.45     |

## *The Churchwardens*

Many of the churchwardens have been farmers. James Pember Biggs held office for 45 years and was also a district councillor. Capel Hardwick from Oldstone served for 17 years, and found time to chair the Parish Council as well. Joe Chamberlain held the post for 35 years, combining it with council and fire duties.

| *1905-50* | James Pember Biggs | *Ringfield* | Farmer |
|-----------|--------------------|-------------|--------|
| *1920-37* | Capel T Hardwick | *Oldstone* | Farmer |
| *1937-53* | George Lancelot Biggs | *West Villas* | Railway clerk |
| *1950-85* | Alfred R Chamberlain | *Orchard Lodge* | Gardener/ fireman |
| *1953-59* | Stanley C Hardwick | *Oldstone* | Farmer |
| *1959-64* | Richard E Biggs | *Ringfield* | Farmer |
| *1964-70* | Henry W Pain | *School House* | Headteacher |
| *1970-89* | Colonel Tom J Hill | *Common Hill* | Soldier |
| *1985-88* | Derrick Brown | *Tyler's Croft* | Software consultant |
| *1988 on* | Gina Children | *Wessington* | Company director |
| *1989-96* | Kevin G Mason | *Old Rectory* | surveyor |
| *1996 on* | Tony Corby | *Pippins* | postmaster |
| *from diocesan records, PCC minutes, trade directories* | | | |

James Pember Biggs was the people's warden – a short, sturdy, elderly man with a wonderfully even temper, good sense of humour and utterly devoted Christian.  He never spoke unkindly of anyone and no-one spoke unkindly of him.  He did a tour of inspection round the church every day

George Lancelot Biggs was the vicar's warden … a large man with an untidy white moustache and a nature that could be surly, but if he took to you he was loyalty itself and showed a humorous and talkative side.  He was a railway porter at Holme Lacy station.

*Memoirs of Wilf Chignell 1956*

Richard Biggs 1977

*Hereford Times*

### Joe Chamberlain Churchwarden/Chorister

Tall, frail Joe Chamberlain, the dearly loved churchwarden, singing with all his might.  No-one would know his ankle is still painful.  Last Sunday, with typical concern, he waited at the lych-gate for Auntie Mary, our oldest inhabitant, to help her up the icy path.  She wisely stayed at home.  He slipped instead!  But a broken ankle won't keep him from the carol service or from reading the lesson.

*from 'A Herefordshire Christmas', by D Green, pub Alan Sutton 1993*
*Jill Howard Jones*

124

## Church Music

The School's head doubled up as church organist and choirmaster till Harry Procter retired in 1943. Since then organists have included Michael Pugh, Helena Biggs and Kevin Mason. The Church was able to provide a free house in Brockhampton in the 1960s to attract organists. Ray Howard Jones recalls that John Bates and Peter Wright had both been cathedral organists.

---

**ORGANIST & CHOIRMASTER 1947**

remuneration £26 per annum play the organ at Sunday morning and evening services, Christmas Day, Good Friday, and, by arrangment at confirmation, wedding and funeral services, weekly Choir Practice, may be after Sunday Evening Service. Two free Sundays during year to be arranged,

entitled to charge extra fee for weddings and funerals, responsible to the Incumbent who delegates to him control of the Choir and Music

*written agreement Parochial Church Council minutes 1947*

---

Choir 1956                                                                                          *P Leyman*

The Vicar wanted to pay choristers in 1942 but was out-voted by the *Parochial Church Council*. George Biggs, a churchwarden and chorister, led the opposition. Choir outings were perhaps compensation. They were in place by 1923 and continued into the 1950s with Weston- super-Mare and Barry amongst the popular destinations, with even longer trips to The Mumbles (170 mile trip). School closed for the day – a Monday or Thursday each August. Two coaches were hired from Midland Red in 1946 at a cost of £17.

"The annual choir outing to the sea. There were usually two coaches, one an enclosed coach and the other a charabanc, this had a canvas top which could be pushed back to make it a large open vehicle, and the most popular with us youngsters."

*Lionel Biggs, b 1925, 2006*

Choir about 1960          *P Leyman*

Wilf Chignell revived the *Choral Society* in 1954 which had been established in the 1900s by Frederick Nott. Helena Biggs recalled singing with them at the *Welsh Eisteddfod* in Swansea. Chignell also introduced several villagers, including Richard E Biggs, to the *Hereford Choral Society*.

Bellringers 1978          *D Biggs*

The **Mothers Union**, one of the longest serving organisations had been formed by 1894, and was open to church- goers 'admitted' at a service by the Vicar. Meetings were held in the Vicarage with the incumbent's wife normally the 'enrolling member'. In the 1970s Union meetings included outside speakers, prayers and bring-and-buy stall as well as trips to other M.U. events. They met in members' homes, often at May Bourne's at Whiterdine. Other active members included Rose Leyman and Edith Probyn from Holm View. Numbers declined from 20 or more in 1971 to only 5 to 10 by 1977 – though they joined forces with Woolhope and Holme Lacy. The Union also organised cleaning of the Church. With nobody willing to be 'enrolling member' at the 1978 AGM the nine remaining members decided to *'go into abeyance'* – and have not met since.

FOWNHOPE MILLENNIUM BELL RINGERS
1999 - 2000

- SALLY WILLIAMS - ALISON PASCOE - DENZIL BIGGS - JACKIE PASCOE -
- MARK PASCOE - DAVID PASCOE -

Biggs family ring in the Millennium                    *D Biggs*

## Caring for the building

It took from 1931 to 1934 to raise £2,000 to restore the 600 year old oak spire from the ravages of death watch beetle, replace the oak shingles, restore the tower walls and lower the bells. There were rummage sales, dances, carol singing, and donations from the WI and from most households. Rising costs, claims of lack of consultation and failure to keep correct committee records led to some angry exchanges which rumbled on till 1938. The famous tympanum was moved inside the church in 1935 to protect it from the weather. The church-yard was extended in 1952, and the lych-gate erected in 1953.

127

"Fownhope decided to celebrate Queen Elizabeth's Coronation with a permanent reminder ... a committee of 19 under Dr G. R. Malkin raised £253 to build a lych-gate, so designed that it could also have seats and be used as a bus shelter. The design was by John Soulsby, the assistant County Architect who lived in Fownhope. The builders Jack and Charlie Stone, together with Harold Pritchard and Bill Jones, worked magnificently, aided by several volunteers ... old stone slats bought from near Eardisley ... not a single nail was used."

*Memoirs of Rev Wilf Chignell, Vicar 1948-56*

Gates were erected on the southern entrance to the memory of Mabel Fox in 1955. Plans for a second lychgate here in 1968 never proceeded. The clock was repaired in 1980. An appeal raised £25,000 in 1993 for new lighting and a gas fired heating system to replace the inefficient solid fuel system. Fund-raising events included a barbecue, barn dance, and concerts.

Oldway Chapel

*J Hardwick*

### Oldway Baptist Chapel

The Baptist chapel had been built in 1826 at Oldway to serve Fownhope, Woolhope and Brockhampton, complete with a Goff's school. The School closed in 1860s but the chapel played an important part in community with several shopkeepers and farmers prominent, as well as the Grundy and Stone families.

> **Fownhope Baptist Church.** The Young People's Society held their New Year Social on Thursday when a crowded school-room testified to the popularity of these meetings, and to the great esteem in which their President, Mrs Barker, is held. Unfortunately, through ill-health, Mrs Barker is leaving the neighbourhood. A splendid spread of refreshments was partaken of, and songs and recitations were given. Mr Kingsbury contributed a farewell song composed for the occasion, after which games were indulged; and so ended a most enjoyable evening.
>
> *Hereford Times, Jan 1921*

I spent my early Sundays attending Oldway Baptist Chapel – morning service, Sunday School in the afternoon and service again in the evening – on occasions it was 'boring' but according to my father it was the 'done thing' – nothing else was done on a Sunday – I wasn't allowed to knit, sew, cut my nails, wash my hair etc.

There were some happy times – the annual anniversary in May, Sunday School anniversary in July, the trip to the seaside when a bus was hired and we took our swim things and picnic lunch, and back on the bus singing songs and hymns on the way. I joined the choir, helped with the Sunday School and played the organ when Mrs James the usual organist was unable to attend.

The churchyard has a great number of my family buried there – the Watkins, Powells, Williams and Biggs.

*Dru Powell née Watkins*

William Barker, Frederick Blackaby, Hugh Lloyd, Alfred Cole and William H Jones were resident pastors in the 1920s and 1930s. Thomas Plumley lived at the Manse in the late 1930s. The Chapel was served by non-resident pastors until John James came in the late 1940s. Havelock Roderick, a retired Welsh minister, lived in The Manse from about 1953 to 1973.

## Rev. Havelock Roderick

remembered for his Welsh voice, long prayers, and the increasing redness of his face as he led the service. Sometimes Lay Preachers came to Oldway. One remembers being told by Roderick: *"Young man, I always say if you don't strike oil in 20 minutes, stop boring!"*

*Rev David V Clarke 2006*

The Baptist congregation dwindled, ecumenical links with Anglican colleagues increased and with some reluctance the decision was taken to close in 1991. The Manse was sold and the church converted to a house though the burial ground remains.

## The Plymouth Brethen

The Meeting House in Ferry Lane was built in 1856 for the Plymouth Brethren. We know very little else about the people involved or their activities at the meeting house. It is believed that Quakers may also have met there. Chris Over ran a successful Sunday School in the late 1970s. A youth club met here in the late 1980s when the county- supported club in the village was struggling. There was a 'happy hour' for pensioners in the 1990s. The meeting house was sold in 2002 for conversion to homes – the attached cottage has been made a holiday home complete with swimming pool!

Oldway Chapel 1990          *D V Clarke*   Brethren meeting house 2006      *M Clark*

## Nuns at Fownhope Court

Fownhope Court was the war-time home for the Community of Saint Mary an 'enclosed order' of Anglican Benedictine Nuns who returned to Malling Abbey in Kent in 1945. The Community published their history in 2006 with memories from Sister (later Mother) Perpetua.

> *'At Fownhope conditions were difficult … record number of illnesses – possibly because of a contaminated water supply. Sister Lucy was buried in Fownhope churchyard on 3rd July 1943, the Community following the coffin in procession.*
> *It happened that the funeral coincided with manoeuvres of a company of the Black Watch and the Home Guard in the main street. They lined both sides of the street and stood at attention as the coffin passed with bayonets reversed and saluted. Not a nun raised her eyes and Sister Osyth heard one say admiringly: "There's order for you!"*
> *We were watched with interest from behind the curtains of many village homes. Mrs Brown had closed the Post Office for the occasion.'*
> Living Stones – the Story of Malling Abbey' 2005 – Shelagh Donnelly

# HEART OF OAK and CLUB WALK

The *Amicable Society, formed* back in 1791 and re-formed in 1876 as the *Heart of Oak Friendly Society*, provided help to sick and unemployed members as well as funeral expenses. No accounts have survived. The Society had 120 members in 1926 *(109 in 1938)*, with £100 annual income from members, and £4,000 *(£4705 in 1938)* in the accounts. The President was the retired doctor, Edgar Averay Jones. The Society paid out £135 in benefits in 1936 but only received £100 in contributions.

Club walk 1922                                                                                 *J Soulsby*

The *Society* owned the four Parsley Row (*now Stony Row*) cottages. In 1941 the new Trustees ( *Reuben J Stone, builder, Albert G Godsell smallholder, and Harry Pugh, publican*) sold two of the cottages to one of the sitting tenants (*Edward Mason*) for £160, little more than they had paid in 1902. If they'd hung on the Society might have become very wealthy – one of the cottages *albeit much improved*) sold in early 2006 for £235,000.

The *Friendly Society* was wound up in 1989, monies were distributed to members, and a new *Heart of Oak Society* formed with the object of keeping the annual *ClubWalk* day alive and fostering community spirit.

Club walk 1922                                                    *W Lewis*

## *The Club Walk*

The *Club Walk*, founded in 1838, suspended during the war, was revived in 1921, and has continued, with a break in the second world war. The Club walk followed a familiar pattern – walk from the New inn to the Church for a short service, addressed by the Vicar, procession with calls at the vicarage, the doctor's house, Mona, next door at Stone House and Morney Cross or the Court, with dinner at the Green Man, and sports in the evening on a field at Mill Farm. In later years the MP, J P L Thomas, presided at the dinner.

Children 1922                                                    *C Sayce*

Club walk 1922 *J Soulsby*

Club walk 1927 *J Soulsby*

**FOWNHOPE**
**HEART OF OAK FRIENDLY SOCIETY**
are holding
**CLUB WALK and DINNER**
at the GREEN MAN HOTEL
*On THURSDAY 21 MAY 1931*
Church at 11 a.m   Dinner at 1.30 p.m.
Chair will be taken by J. P. L. Thomas Esq.
BERRY HILL FULL SILVER BAND and
Peter's Roundabouts.  Shooting Galleries
etc.  A good Sports Programme
F.  JONES SECRETARY

*Hereford Times notice May 1931*

Club walk 1935 *D Biggs*

The Walk was revived in 1946 –

"Every year the members assemble outside the *Green Man* and march up to the Church led by a band, usually the *Lydbrook Brass Band* and their large *Friendly Society* banner … the members (then) march round to the vicarage … the band played two or three tunes … going (on) to some of the bigger houses, where they played and wished the inhabitants good health, and were refreshed with free drink … lunch in the *Village Hall* with speeches and more beer.

In the afternoon there were sports and a fair, and in the evening, a dance. Fownhope was pretty tired by the end, but this made no difference to the excellent congregations next day."

*Rev Wilfred R Chignell, Vicar 1948 -56*

Club walk 1952                    *W Lewis*

Bows 1950s          *M Andrews*

Henry Jauncey 1950s          *P Leyman*

| Heart of Oak Club Walk & Sports 7 June 1958 | | |
|---|---|---|
| Church Parade | Lunch | Sports |
| 10.40 am | 1.30 pm | 3 pm |

Club sports 1957

*D Brown*

Club walk doctor's house 1963

*J Hardwick*

Octogenarian takes part in Club Walk, Fownhope Friendly Society's annual event. Mr. Frank Godsell aged 80, the oldest member who joined at the age of 6 took part in the 82nd Club Walk on Saturday. Also taking part were his cousins, Mr. Walter Godsell aged 75 and Mr. Albert Godsell aged 83 who are brothers. The walk created as much interest as ever and attracted many interested spectators. Large numbers of children and adults watched members of the Society and Lydbrook Silver Prize Band preparing to move off from the Green Man Inn. A member held the traditional branch of an oak tree at the head of the gathering.

Following the oak branch came two members carrying the Society's banner with the motto "Unity is Strength". Members of the society held staves with bright bunches of flowers fixed to them and marched to Fownhope church for the traditional short service.

The Rev. H. Roderick, Minister of Fownhope Baptist Church who preached said the Society contributed a sense of belonging to the community and performed splendid service. He was pleased to see young members taking part in the procession. *"It all depends on the members of the younger generation whether the world achieves universal peace."* The service was conducted by the vicar, the Reverend H. C. Sell and Mr. D. Dance was organist.

After the service members went to the vicarage to meet the vicar's wife and family and to enjoy light refreshments. Their visit to the vicarage over, the members moved to the house of the village doctor, Dr. G. R. Malkin. Members of the band and the society and villagers accepted glasses of cider, beer and lemonade and hear Dr. Malkin say he hoped the society would go from strength to strength. The procession reformed and marched to the home of Mr. Francis L. Pym, a county councillor. The procession moved on to Whitegates, the home of Mr. I. Barclay and then returned to the village.

Members of the society, band and guests later enjoyed an excellent lunch in the village hall at which Mr. F. L. Pym presided. After grace, said by the vicar, Mr. Pym proposed a toast *"Success and prosperity to the Society"*. The aims and objectives of the Society, Mr. Pym thought, were admirable. They were worthy of the trouble taken to produce such an effective gathering *"The product of real Fownhope village life."* Today the society was on a sound financial footing and giving members of the younger generation something they could live up to. Mr. P. Pocknell, replying, said the society could boast assets of £7,000 and had a junior members account of £497. Mr. L. Alford proposed a toast to the Chairman and a toast to the visitors was proposed by Mr. C. Patterson. Mr. Roderick responded. After lunch sports were organised in Whiterdine fields and an amusement fair, close by, aroused much enjoyment. Mr. Neville Barnett, musical director, was in charge of the band.

*Hereford Times 13 June 1958*

*Edmund F Gange, aged 88, at Club Walk 1955 talking to 5 year old David Gilbert*

Club walk 1983                    *M Andrews*

The walk has often been held in conjunction with other celebrations. In 1953 it was combined with the opening of the lych-gate to celebrate the Coronation when 250 packed into the Church. The Silver Jubilee was the feature in 1977 with skittles and darts competitions, six-a-side football, discos, dance, and over 60s party, and planting of trees, and new seats. The Green Man's 500th anniversary of Green Man was noted in 1985 while the 1993 walk was combined with fund-raising for Church lighting and open gardens and a guided walk. Fund-raising for the Church was combined with a flower festival in 2000 which featured the *Talgarth Male Voice choir* concert, jazz concert, and a barbecue at Stone House. 2002 was an opportunity to celebrate the *Golden Jubilee* with the dedication of the new play area on the Recreation Field, funded by the Society, and presentation of mugs, sports, party and a dance.

Club walk 2005  John Hardwick & Denzil Biggs          *M Clark*

The Society has also organised the village Bonfire and Fireworks in November, with the involvement of the Leisure Centre in more recent years.

Club walk 2005                                                      *M Clark*

## Ancient Order Of Foresters

Two other friendly societies were active in the village. The *Court and Wyeside AOF* had the patronage of the Herefords at Sufton and Lechmeres at Fownhope Court, and met at the *Moon* in Mordiford. They held their Club Day with a Walk and Feast each June, often walking from the Moon to Fownhope Church. They had invested in local property – the three cottages and the blacksmith's shop in Ferry Lane near to the Post Office.

---

Friendly Society Church Parade at Fownhope

Despite the inclement weather on Sunday, about 100 members of the Foresters met at the headquarters of Court Wyeside, the Moon Inn Mordiford, where they were joined by the Fownhope Heart of Oak Society and members of other societies and marched to Fownhope where, at the parish church, a service was conducted and the Rev. F. G. Nott preached … met by the Hereford City Band and played through the village. collection amounted to £3 16s 8d for the General Hospital.

*Hereford Times 31 July 1920*

---

The Fownhope Lodge of the *Royal Antediluvian Order of Buffaloes* organised several well-attended dances and whist drives in the Memorial Hall in the 1940s to raise funds for ambulances. They also held lodge meetings on a Sunday afternoon in the Green Man.

# MEMORIAL HALL and CLUBS

Social events were held in the pubs or the School until the Hall was erected in 1920. A Sling Hut used by New Zealand troops was bought for £1338, carried from Salisbury Plain, and re-erected next to the School on land donated by the Lechmere family as a memorial to the twelve men who had lost their lives in the war. Mabel Fox donated 300 sixpences which were used by people to make money- one 'lass' bought eggs with her sixpence, and donated the income from the sale of the new-born chicks.

Panto 1925                                                                *J Soulsby*

The Hall provided a valuable space, and led to many new clubs and activities in the village. It was used for dances, whist drives, club events, cookery and dairy classes, and public meetings. There was even a travelling theatre in 1928. A piano was installed. A caretaker was paid £3 15s a year in 1927 – £39 by 1961.

FOWNHOPE MEMORIAL HALL.
Grand
**HOLIDAY DANCE**
AUGUST MONDAY
9 p.m. to 1 a.m.
AMBASSADORS BAND
Bus leaves Bounds' car park 8.30 p.m., returning after dance.     5891

Old hall 1986                                                         *J Soulsby*

Dances were an important feature in post-war years with old time and modern dances. Dances would normally run from 8 or 9pm till midnight, 1am on New Year's Eve, with buses from Hereford. The bands included such exotic names as Mighty Atoms, Reg Chad's Band, Golden Linnetts, Diamond Players, Romany Players and the Berry Hill Silver Band. Admission was 2s 6d (*12 and a half pence*) – 3s for New Years Eve, with proceeds to the Club Walk, Hall funds, the children's Christmas Treat, RAOB and the Oswestry hospital.

Saturday, December 5, a Dance in aid of the London Distress Fund at Fownhope Memorial Hall
Swing Time Dance Band        Dancing 9-1,      admission 1/6d.      Forces 1s.
Refreshments, moderate charges Next Dance, Boxing night, December 26
*Hereford Times, Nov 1940*

Facilities in the Hall were limited. Water had to be carried from nearby wells until a tank took rainwater off the roof in 1942. A septic tank was installed in 1932 but capacity was limited to one cubic yard. The drains could not cope with washing up water from war-time cookery classes. The village doctor, Godfrey Malkin, concerned about safety, asked for improvements to the electrics in 1942.

Knitting for victory! 1942                                    *B Snape*

## Hall Charges 1956

| | parishioners | non-parishioners |
|---|---|---|
| The Managers decided that local hirers should pay less for the use of the Hall | | |
| *per hour* | *3s 6d (17.5p)* | *5s (25p)* |
| *dances/concerts* | *30s (£1.50)* | *30s (£1.50)* |
| *whist drives* | *20s (£1)* | *25s (£1.25)* |
| *dinners/lunches* | *30s (£1.50)* | *40s (£2)* |

*Weddings 40s, jumble 30s, evening classes 3s6d p hr;*
*film shows 5s p hr badminton/youth club/clinic/WI 10s 6d*

## Hall Users 1929-70

A wide range of clubs and users -some clubs used the School, Chapels, a Pub or met in homes

| | | | |
|---|---|---|---|
| Badminton | 1947-70 | Pros & cons party | 1929-30 |
| Bellringers | 1934-54 | RAOB (Buffaloes) | 1939-50 |
| British Legion | 1929-70 | Red Cross | 1942 & 56 |
| Church choir | 1946-9 | Rest centre | 1944 |
| church PCC | 1934-70 | School | 1939-70 |
| Clinic | 1953-70 | Scouts/cubs | 1956-70 |
| Conservatives | 1927-57 | St John's ambulance | 1935 |
| Darby & Joans | 1969-70 | Tennis club dance | 1933-42 |
| Eisteddfod | 1934 | Women's Institute | 1927-70 |
| Evacuees | 1940-1 | Young people's assoc | 1935-49 |
| Flower Show | 1943 & 45 | Youth club | 1943-70 |
| Football Club | 1929-45 | Young wives | 1970 |
| Girl Guides | 1955-58 | Army cadet corps | 1969-70 |
| Girls Friendly Soc | 1927-35 | *Classes* | |
| Heart Of Oak | 1948-58 | Basketry | 1952 |
| Home Guard | 1940-44 | Cookery classes | 1935-9 |
| Land Army | 1944 | Dairy classes | 1937 |
| Liberals | 1931-56 | Dance classes | 1951 |
| Men's Club | 1929-54 | Dressmaking | 1952-6 |
| Mothers Union | 1929-70 | Gym/ PT classes | 1935-8 |
| Observer Corps | 1941-47 | *Outside groups* | |
| Oldway Chapel | 1939-70 | Brockhampton football | 1949-55 |
| Parish Council | 1969-70 | Holme Lacy cricket | 1948-49 |
| Pre-school playgroup | 1970 | Woolhope Young Farmers | 1969-70 |

The Hall was managed by a committee of nine elected by an annual public meeting, *(normally a Saturday evening)* with people from the Church, the Baptists, a farmer, a trader, a lady to represent girls using the Hall, and four others. It was not an ideal arrangement. Disputes between the committee and the trustees were finally resolved in 1969 when the Charity Commissioners imposed a 'model' constitution with trustees from each current user groups – the Church, Baptists, Parish Council, Mothers Union, young wives, WI, army cadet corps, Darby & Joans, British Legion, pre-school playgroup, youth club and Young Farmers, and three others elected at the public meeting. Membership has altered as user groups have changed.

## *New Hall For Old?*

A survey in 1970 found that users were concerned of the lack of space, heating, and kitchen facilities, and the difficulty keeping the Hall clean. The Hall committee tried valiantly to tackle the problems in the 1970s and installed a new floor. The WI and Youth Club re-decorated the Hall. However by the 1980s it was clear that the Hall was inadequate for the demands of a growing and discerning community.

Preparing new Hall                                                    *M Best*

The Parish Council proposed in 1984 that a new hall should be built by Scotch Firs to provide more space, including parking and tennis courts. There were strong objections from 32 nearby residents, led by Sydney Trenchard Morgan and John Gill. A local poll supported the scheme but it was turned down by the planners on highway grounds. The Parish Council was advised that an appeal could cost them £5,000, so decided to re-build on the existing site. The old hall was demolished in October 1986.

## The New Hall

The new hall was opened in October 1987, at a cost of £150,000 with £65,000 from the Parish Council, £30,000 from the county council, £20,000 from the Sports Council, and £40,000 from local fund-raising organised by Michael Best, including a lottery, bingo and auctions. The design was modelled on a traditional Herefordshire barn, with space for 200 people (140 set out with tables), film shows, dances, and height for badminton and indoor tennis. A kitchen, toilets, cloakroom and storage were included, together with an upstairs committee room. The building was opened by the new vicar, Ralph Garnett, Brig. John Foley for the Legion, Dr Patrick Ramage, chair of the Parish Council, and John Seeley chairman of the Hall committee. Further improvements were made in 2005 with improved kitchen, toilets and storage facilities.

Hall 2006

*A Corby*

| Parish Council £65,000 | Donations & fund-raising £40,000 |
| --- | --- |
| | County Council £30,000 |
| | Sports Council £20,000 |

## Clubs & Groups

The Hall stimulated new activities. The **Flower Club** was set up in 1981 with monthly speakers and demonstrations of flower arranging in the Hall. Since 1985 it has organised four flower festivals in the Church. The 2000 festival, led by Shirley Green, chairperson since 1997, attracted 1200 visitors in a weekend, and raised £4617.

Shirley Green flower club 2002          *Flower Club*

The new Hall and Recreation Pavilion have helped to spark new activities. There were film shows. A sports club was set up to provide for badminton and five-a-side football, with plans for basketball too. The **Bowls Club** was set up by John Merritt and Norman Allen in 1988 to play short mat bowls in the Hall. The Club has been a leading member of the county association, chaired by Fred Jolley, has won the county league title, and had six members in the county team that won the English championship in 2004. It now has 28 members from a wide area, has four mats, and plays twice a week in the Hall.

Bowls 2006          *Bowls Club*

Patrick Ramage helped to set up the **Garden Club** in 1996 with monthly meetings in the Hall in winter, and garden visits and barbecue in summer. Membership has stood at around 50-60. The club exhibited at Chelsea and planted daffodils round the parish in 1999. In 2001, with the Flower Club, it revived the celebrated village Flower and Vegetable Show after a lapse of almost 60 years.

Party 1989                                    *Jane Davies*

Table Tennis was revived after a lapse of 20 years. Don Parry set up the **Leisure Five O Club** in 1997 to cater for middle-aged tastes, with a mixture of speakers, and outdoor events, including canoeing, barbecue and visits. Membership swiftly reached 100, and grew to 133. The group also set up 'Flicks in the Sticks' films programme in the Hall in winter months.

Leisure Five O            *Ann Corby*   Flicks in the Sticks            *S Gough*

The **Bridge Club** founded in 1992 in Faulkner House, meets weekly in the new River Bed Restaurant. The **Art Group**, setup in 2000, meets in the Pavilion, and shows in the annual art exhibition in the Hall. **Friends Of Fownhope** came into being in 1996 to conserve Fownhope's rural character, re-formed in 2002 as the Residents Association which has also published leaflets of local walks. The **Walkers** group was formed by Maurice Spratt in 2004 with a monthly programme of local walks plus 'Health walks'. Fred Jolley set up the **Dance** Club in 2005 which meets weekly for a tea dance in the Hall.. and we must find space for the **Local History Group**, formed in 2005, who researched and published this book!

Art exhibition in Hall 2006 *S Gough*

To have so many organisations in the parish of this size seems remarkable – and some have not survived. The Women's Institute went into abeyance though some of its role has been taken on by the Leisure Five O club.

## *Political Parties*

The Conservatives were very active in the 1920s. Their AGM in 1926 lists several village notables including Dr Averay Jones, Edmund Gange of The Folly, and Albert Stone of Pennybrook who passed the chair to William Hill of Rise Cottage. For a time there were separate branches for men and women, the latter led by Florence St Barbe of Rock House. They drew 100 to a meeting in the Hall in1927, and had regular whist drives. JPL Thomas, who regained the seat for the Conservatives in 1931, had spent some childhood holidays at Rock House, and found time to get to many of the Club Walks in his twenty years as MP. There was a Young Conservative branch for short time in the late 1950s which involved Michael Williams and Brian Chamberlain. The Conservative branch folded in 1997.

The Liberals held social events, including a dance, in the Hall, and used the School for election meetings. Though less active in the village they had some success at the polls. Frank Owen won the seat for the Liberals in 1929 at the age of 24, made his name later as a journalist, like another candidate, Robin Day, whose election address in 1959 featured a shot of him with Sam Warren at Joans Hill.

## CLUBS & ACTIVITIES 1919-2007

| 1919 | 1945-58 | 2007 | |
|---|---|---|---|
| (Cricket) | (Cricket) | Cricket | Garden Club |
| (Flower Show) | Flower Show | Flower Club | Cubs |
| Church | Church | Church | Walkers |
| Church Choir | Church Choir | Church Choir | Football |
| HOS/Club Walk | HOS/Club Walk | HOS/Club Walk | Leisure Five O |
| Parish Council | Parish Council | Parish Council | Residents |
| Vestry | PCC | PCC | Recreation Field |
| Voluntary Library | County Library | Mobile Library | History Group |
| Baptist Chapel | Baptist Chapel | British Legion | Indigo |
| Foresters | Foresters | Bowls | Ballet Class |
| Girls Friendly Soc | AYPA/Youth | Bridge | Playgroup |
| (11) | British Legion | Badminton | Tae Kwondo |
| | Choir Outing | Bellringers | Art Group |
| | Conservatives | Dance Club | WRVS |
| | Liberals | Brownies | Scouts |
| | Memorial Hall | Memorial Hall | Table Tennis |
| | Mens Club | | (32) |
| | Mothers Union | | |
| | WI | | |
| | Badminton | | |
| | Bellringers | | |
| | Buffaloes | | |
| | Dances | | |
| | Guides | | |
| | Observer Corps | | |
| | Orchestra | | |
| | Red Cross | | |
| | Scouts | | |
| | Tennis | | |
| | (29) | | |

## Some Events

The **Fownhope Flower show** was a major event in the years before the 1914 war. It was revived in 1937 by Joe Chamberlain and Harry Lloyd. The event on August Bank holiday Monday, was held on Morney meadow loaned by Capel Hardwick, attracted 3,000 visitors, and raised £50 towards the much needed recreation field. Buses were put on from Hereford and Ross. The Newent Silver Band played, there was a Punch and Judy show, and Doreen Thomas was crowned carnival queen. The 1939 show was an equally grand event:

Tenders required for Wet and Dry Canteen, Band, Marquees, Radio car. Ground to let for ices, sweets, amusements, clay pigeon shooting etc., schedules apply to A. R. Chamberlain, Orchard Cottage, Fownhope. Tenders to General Secretary, H. Lloyd, Fownhope. Motor cycle and cycle entry forms now ready. Apply to D. Leyman, Sports Secretary, Stone House, Fownhope.

**There was no outdoor show in 1940 but an indoor event was held in 1943.**

The flower show took place at the Memorial Hall on Bank Holiday Monday afternoon and between 300 and 400 persons spent a very pleasant time.

The various exhibits, the childrens' sports and the side shows provided interest and entertainment for old and young alike. Mrs. Cocke and the many friends and helpers who assisted in making the show a success are to be congratulated on the result of their efforts which provided a net sum of about £20 for division between a childrens' playing field fund and a comforts fund for the RAF.

The judges of the exhibits which were open to the parishes of Mordiford, Holme Lacey, Brockhampton, Woolhope and Sollershope as well as Fownhope were Mr. Husbands of Upton Bishop and Mr. Lewis of Brockhampton. Mrs. Dane acted as judge of the flower displays, Mrs. Blain of war-time jam and Miss White of the children's drawings.

There were races and other items in the children's sports. The vicar, the Rev. C. T. Cottrell acted as sportsmaster and valuable assistance in the arrangements was given by Messrs. C. Godsell and B. Lloyd., The sideshows were well patronised and those in charge of the refreshments did capital business. The prize winners in the flower and vegetable show were as follows:
Peas: 1. H. Lloyd, 2. A. Brown, 3. C. Howells   Broad beans: 1. A. H. Jackson
Runner beans: 1. J. C. Howells, 2. H. Lloyd, 3. A. H. Jackson
Onions (winter): 1. A. H. Jackson, 2. Mrs. Nicholls, 3. A. Brown
Onions (spring): l. J. C. Howells, 2. H. Lloyd, 3. A. H. Jackson
Eschallots: 1. Mrs. Prince, 2. H. Lloyd, 3. R. Wesley
Potatoes (kidney): 1. J. C. Howells, 2. J. Williams, 3. Mrs. T. Godsell
Round: 1. F. Godsell, 2. Vera Biggs, 3. Mrs. Malkin   Parsnips: C. Pocknell
Round Beet: 1. J. C. Howells, 2. George Wood, 3. F. Godsell
Vegetable marrows: 1. Geo Wood, 2. F. Godsell, 3. C. Pocknell
Table decoration: 1. Rosalie Godsell, 2. Mrs. Malkin
War-time jam: 1. Mrs. Seabourne, 2. Mrs. Lloyd Bowens, 3. Mrs. Godsell
Wildflowers (children under 14 years) 1. Jean Wallis, 2. Colin Curtis 3. John Pritchard
Sweet peas: 1. J. C. Howells, 2. J. Williams   Plums: J. H. Lloyd, Mrs. Malkin
Apples: 1. Mrs. Malkin, 2. A. Brown, 3. A. H. Jackson   Pears: Mrs. Malkin

The first prize for the best drawings by children was won by Colin Curtis, the second by Bryan Chamberlain, the third by Charles Seabourne and a fourth was awarded to Kenneth Davies. Mrs. Carter of Brockhampton gave an interesting display of bottled fruits and vegetables and Mrs. Fox gave beautiful flowers for decoration which were tastefully arranged by Mr. Chamberlain and Mr. Vaughan who were also largely responsible for the arrangement of the exhibits.

Television made very little impact in the post war years. Most people travelled by bus to the cinema in Hereford, or made their own entertainment. There were some remarkable achievements.

Orchestra 1954

*J Soulsby*

### Fownhope Orchestra 1952

Wilf Chignell set up a village orchestra in 1952, followed by a choral society in 1954

"It would be fun to get a toy orchestra together and give a performance of Haydn's *Toy Symphony* at a village concert. We rehearsed madly in more senses than one. The orchestra went into action for the village concert, gave performances at Brockhampton and Madley and went to Birmingham one memorable day to appear on T.V.! We travelled by train ... our trumpeters Dick Biggs and Michael Pugh ate enormous meals ... we went to the B.B.C. and then to Bingley Hall where the performance was to take place. This was the first outside T.V. programme done on Midlands TV. and was the Hall cold! It was February!

We were a seven and half minute appearance. We were entertained to tea and received a fee of £20 which covered our cost of travel. The orchestra looked splendid (but) at no time was the whole orchestra – only 14 strong – seen at once.

We played the last movement and it went pretty well but Mary Soulsby's *ocarina* seemed to make hardly any sound – back on the train she examined it, there stuck in the instrument was a small bit of silver paper, she had had a bar of chocolate in this pocket!"

*Memoirs of Rev Wilfred R Chignell, Vicar 1948-56*

## Tom Spring Pageant 1954

Tom Winter *aka* Tom Spring, son of a village butcher, had been all-England's champion bare knuckle fighter in the 1820s. Tom Robbins from Rudge End Farm and AV Lucas suggested that he should be remembered in his home parish. A committee chaired by Godfrey Malkin agreed to a memorial, built by Stone Brothers, on the site of his birthplace – the now deserted Wych End Farm off Woolhope Road. The memorial was dedicated by JPL Thomas, MP, in August 1954, supported by a massive pageant of folk dancing, archery, fencing, gymnastics, music and prize fighting. The School and Fownhope and Woolhope WIs put on a re-enactment of Tom's life. Tom was played by Vic Powell and Michael Williams. There was a floral dance through the village, and a dance in the Hall.

Tom Spring event 1954          *D Grant*

## SMART Dramatics 1993-2001

St Mary's Amateur Rural Theatre, formed in 1993 under the aegis of the *Parochial Church Council*, was the idea of Michael Best to put on music /drama productions to raise money for the Church heating and lighting appeal. There were nine productions in the Church between 1993 and 2001, involving 50 players, aged from 4 to 70, drawn from the surrounding area, under the direction of Richard Errington, Ann Brown, Kevin Mason and Margaret Skelton.

SMART theatre                                                                      *R Best*

The productions were: *A Grain of Mustard Seed, Captain Noah and his Floating Zoo, Joseph and his Amazing Technicolour Dreamcoat, Autumn Enchantment, Greater than Gold, Godspell, While Shepherds Watched, Switched on SMART,* and *The Selfish Giant.*

# THE WOMEN'S INSTITUTE

The new hall helped to bring new groups into being. One of the first was the *Women's Institute*, set up in 1923 – one of several in the county – based on ideas from rural Canada! Most villages had one by 1930s – though Fownhope with 100 members was much larger than the county average of 25 members.

*"to provide for fuller education of countrywomen in citizenship, public questions, both national and international, music, drama, and other cultural subjects, instruction and training in agriculture, handicrafts, domestic science, health and social welfare."*

Early press reports stress *citizenship* – a talk from the Director of Education, *democracy* – with ballots for committee places – and *domestic skills*. Mabel Fox from Orchard Cottage, the first lady JP, was a driving force, and active in the *Rural Community Council* that had close links with WI movement.

WI pageant 1948                                                                 *D Brown*

"I became one of the Founder Members.
In those days the Institute was geared more towards useful instructional lectures; classes were held for dressmaking, glove, slipper and toy making. More elaborate instruction in upholstery, quilting, together with advanced cookery and a high standard in icing for wedding and Christmas cakes. It was a means of opportunity for women in remote rural areas.
It was not all study, however; we were involved in some wonderful Pageants. I recall one in the grounds of Holme Lacy House.
I was very excited when I attended The Queen's Garden Party at Buckingham Palace when the Golden Jubilee was celebrated."

*Memories of Helena Rose Biggs née Watkins*

# YOUTH GROUPS

The **Girls' Friendly Society** had been in being since at least 1909. Most members were daughters of members of the Mothers' Union. Miss Evans of Ringfield was the GFS's 'associate' in 1927. The Society's Sale of Work and entertainments raised money for the school sports day Lottie Procter, wife of the School's head, helped with handicrafts and sewing, though there was a Ladies or Girls Sewing Guild in the 1920s.

The **Anglican Young People's Association** replaced the GFS, catering for boys and girls. It was normally called the YPA rather than AYPA, perhaps to appeal to the Baptists and non-churchgoers, though there was also a strong Baptists youth group at this time. The YPA had regular bookings, including whist drives in the Memorial Hall and they also met in the Vicarage.

### JOIN THE A Y P A !

When I was young I joined the *Anglican Young Peoples Association*, run by Ruth and Vera Biggs from Cannon House. All the local village youngsters went, and we had a good time. We always sang the song "*Join the AYPA*", and we did dancing. I expect we had a gramophone record. I think it was once a week.

*Renee Thomas talked to Madge Daines and Pam Colley, 2006*

Scouts show

*J Jones snr*

## Youth Club

The Youth Club was formed in 1951 by Rev Wilf Chignell, replacing the church-based *Young Peoples Association*. The Club met in the Hall and had social events and dances. It was open to those over 15 years living within three miles of Fownhope. Chignell's note in the Parish Magazine – *"no rowdies or hooligans* "- may suggest that Fownhope wasn't quite so peaceful then! It was dormant in 1970 and was revived with vigour in 1973 by newcomer John Jones senior with help from the Vicar, Ray Howard Jones and Phillip Bream. Their programme included

* *playing shinty – with borrowed sticks*
* *canoeing, re-conditioned canoes, took part in Hereford to Ross race*
* *tug of war, mixed team, got to the NAYC final at Nottingham*
* converted *fire engine to a coach with help from Richard Biggs at Ringfield (see photo page 124)*
* *helped to decorate the old hall*
* *YC football team won Herefordshire Youth competition – then represented the county to reach the national finals at Goodison Park in 1983*

The Club made use of the Old School when it became available for community use after 1979. The county council set up a youth project in 1995 with a paid youth worker. By 1999 youth club attendances had fallen and the Club went into abeyance – though another youth group continued for some time in the *Brethren chapel* in Ferry Lane.

Guides 1955                                                    *P Leyman*

158

## Scouts and Guides

A troop of Scouts and Guides (led by a Lechmere) is said to have flourished in the 1920s. Both were revived in the 1950s. Wilf Chignell set up a **Scouts** troop in July 1953. He was the approved examiner, pathfinder, stalker, tracker, and guide with Lawrence Wilson from Court Orchard as handyman, and Frances Coleman of Glenridge, Common Hill as first aider. There were 15 scouts in the troop in 1957. Activities included hiking, camp, tests for badges, and Bob-a-Job week which raised £1 6s 6d in 1957. The Camp was held close by at How Caple in 1956 – the menu, four meals each day, was set out in advance for the whole fortnight! Francis Pym from Orchard Cottage was Chairman of the Scouts. He went on to be county councillor, entered parliament and became Foreign Secretary. The Scouts took over the chalet at Woodview from the Guides in 1958, and later used part of Stones' old workshop in Ferry Lane, before moving to the Recreation pavilion.

Mary Soulsby revived the **Girl Guides** in January 1955 with a hike in search of fungus and wildlife, followed at her cottage at Mansells' Ferry by a meal of sausages and tea, made of course with condensed milk! Mary's early logbook records a varied programme ranging from church parades, waste paper collection, tracking on Cherry Hill, and games of rounders. The Guides rented a garden hut at Woodview from Hilda Cooper. There were hikes to Common Hill, Mordiford and to Brockhampton along the river. The first camp was held by the river Wye below Biblins, and included rambles to King Arthur's Caves and to Tintern Abbey. Troops of Cubs and Brownies were formed by 1959, though the Brownies had to be revived in 1976. The Brownies and Guides joined forces for a production of *Cinderella* in 1980.

Cinderella *J Soulsby*

"There were no Brownies in Fownhope but I owe a great debt of gratitude to Mary Soulsby, she was a great influence in my life and John too. The Guiding in Fownhope was phenomenal ... Mary Soulsby introduced me to learning about the countryside ... they owned Mansell's Ferry ... and we used to have camp fires and sleep indoors (there). And it was just wonderful, we all became one family. ... And the quality of things she did. We used to sit quietly in groups for half an hour, perhaps 20 minutes, just listening to country sounds and then we used to record all the things we could hear. And that's what children need. Time to stop and appreciate."

*Jennifer Higham, née Williams, talked to Mandy Dees & Pam Colley 2005*

## Playgroups

The first pre-school playgroup met in the Hall in 1968. There were 27 children on the register by 1980, open three mornings per week, charging 45p a time. Most of the children came from Fownhope (60%) with some from Woolhope and Brockhampton. The Mum and Tots was formed by Jennifer Harris-Mayes from The Stores (*now Cassiobury*) in early 1977. It met in the Ferry Lane chapel and continued to 2001. The playgroup moved in 2002 to a refurbished classroom in the School, next to the reception class, helping to bridge the gap between playgroup and school. Lottery funding of £11,500 paid for much of the refurbishment, as well as a fridge and cooker. This group, supervised by Carolyn Jones for many years, met five mornings each week, and included a lunch club.

Playgroup                                    *Group*    Playgroup at school                          *Group*

# The BRITISH LEGION

The Legion was formed in January 1928 to serve Fownhope and Woolhope, but expanded to take in thirteen parishes centred on Fownhope. The village doctor, ex naval surgeon James Baggs was a founder member, and treasurer until 1934. Richard Biggs held several posts over a 47 year period, including 17 years as President. Richard Dane from Morney Cross was President from 1935 till 1940. Douglas Banks from Hillview by Rudge End was treasurer for 17 years till 1992. Stan Wood has been the standard bearer since the 1970s.

RBL parade 1995

*V Thompson*

The Legion's Armistice Day parades and church service have rotated each November between villages. The Legion has also held a dinner for members before Armistice Day since 1931, generally in Fownhope, and a church parade each July since 1931.

| *Legion Dinner 1931* | | |
|---|---|---|
| *two joints* | *Vegetables* | *sweets* |
| *lamb & beef* | *In Season* | *tarts & custard jellies* |
| | *cheese; biscuits, cress* | |
| caterer – J.Jones the Garrick Hereford 2/6d occasional licence (Green Man and New Inn invited to bid) joint cooked in oven of Mr Hancorn – the baker Entertainer from Hereford | | |

Legion dinner                                        *S Clifford*

A benevolent fund was set up to help war veterans. Sick members have been visited, often by padre clergy. A summer treat for wives and children was held from 1928 to 1939 but not continued. The Legion has lobbied on behalf of ex-service personnel on council housing, pensions, benefits, and raised funds through dances and whist drives. Membership has ranged from 62 to 140 in 2005.

A FOUNDER member of the Fownhope and Woolhope branch of the Royal British Legion, Mr Dick Biggs, a spritely 82 year old, proudly marched with his compatriots to Church on Sunday to celebrate the branch's 50th anniversary. One of the branch's five founder-members of 1927, Mr Biggs has been president for the past 14 years.

A world war veteran he saw front line action with the Royal Garrison Artillery in the trenches at Ypres. Mr Biggs retired from dairy farming 16 years ago. He has sung in the choir for 73 years and taken part in the Three Choirs Festivals since 1939.

*Hereford Times 1976*

Church service with Rev. Will Pridie 2000          *J Banks*

## Royal Observer Corps

The Corps was formed just before the 1939 war to plot aircraft movements, manned 24 hours a day, from a post (24/U3) in Whiterdine, close to the New Inn. The ROC was stood down after the war but continued in a training capacity into the 1960s, first from high ground near Tump Farm, and then from Oldway where it was intended to detect nuclear fall-out! Eighteen people were involved with the Corps at some point, including shopkeeper Harry Lloyd, Richard Biggs, Geoff Longman from the New Inn, Dolly Haines and Lionel Biggs.

Observer corps 1946                                          *L Biggs*

An **Army Cadet Corps** met in the Hall from 1969 to 1974 but wound up through lack of support. It must have been difficult to compete with the Young Farmers and Youth Club at their peak.

# SPORTS and RECREATION

Brockhampton's cricket field dates from 1897, Mordiford's from about 1905, yet Fownhope had to wait till 1993 to get a publicly owned facility. The *Flower Show*, started in 1897, depended on the generosity of a farmer for just two days each August. School sports took a half day in the same month, as did church fetes. The football team, started in 1920, as well as school teams, had more of a problem. Level fields are at a premium here. Hay meadows were not available for early season games, and would be too wet in mid-winter. Other land might be too uneven. So Fownhope's pre-war football team faltered.

Harry Lloyd, shopkeeper at West End Stores, and AR 'Joe' Chamberlain, gardener at Orchard Cottage, revived the annual *Flower Show and Sports* in 1936 on whatever fields they could find, often the Morney meadows near Rock House. They put the profits from the Show into a fund for a community sports field. The *Parish Meeting* in 1959 resolved to turn this dream into reality. The *Parish Council* pursued land at Whiterdine, Bowens and Church Croft. It tried to buy land by agreement, but was also prepared to ask the *District Council* to use their compulsory purchase powers.

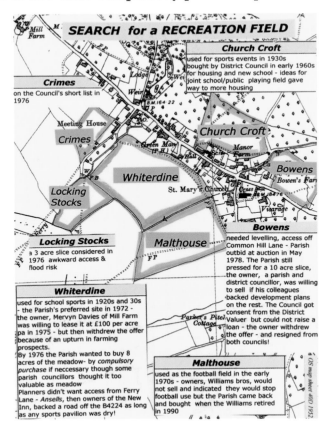

**SEARCH for a RECREATION FIELD**

**Church Croft**
used for sports events in 1930s bought by District Council in early 1960s for housing and new school - ideas for joint school/public playing field gave way to more housing

**Crimes**
on the Council's short list in 1976

**Locking Stocks**
a 3 acre slice considered in 1976 awkward access & flood risk

**Whiterdine**
used for school sports in 1920s and 30s - the Parish's preferred site in 1972 - the owner, Mervyn Davies of Mill Farm was willing to lease it at £100 per acre pa in 1975 - but then withdrew the offer because of an upturn in farming prospects.
By 1976 the Parish wanted to buy 8 acres of the meadow- by *compulsory purchase* if neccessary though some parish councillors thought it too valuable as meadow
Planners didn't want access from Ferry Lane - *Ansells*, then owners of the New Inn, backed a road off the B4224 as long as any sports pavilion was dry!

**Bowens**
needed levelling, access off Common Hill Lane - Parish outbid at auction in May 1978. The Parish still pressed for a 10 acre slice, the owner, a parish and district councillor, was willing to sell if his colleagues backed development plans on the rest. The Council got consent from the District Valuer but could not raise a loan - the owner withdrew the offer - and resigned from both councils!

**Malthouse**
used as the football field in the early 1970s - owners, Williams bros, would not sell and indicated they would stop football use but the Parish came back and bought when the Williams retired in 1990

The Malthouse field, used for football matches since 1972, was sold in 1992 to the Parish Council when the Williams brothers had given up farming. The Recreation Field was formally 'opened' in 1993.

The football club had wanted some changing facilities on the field. Phil Paton, retired local policeman, offered £60,000 for a new pavilion in 1994, on the proviso that there should be no fruit machines. The newly formed *Recreation Field Club* came forward with proposals for a £600,000 scheme in 1996 which prompted a period of frenzied debate which divided the community. Plans were revised, and a two storey pavilion opened in 1999. The Parish Council leased the field (and pavilion) to the Recreation Field Club in 2000. Facilities were enhanced two years with the opening of the Jubilee play area, funded in part by the Heart of Oak Society.

Pavilion 2006 *D M Clark*   Football on recreation field 2006 *D M Clark*

## Football

We have photographs of the Fownhope football team in 1921/22 but no reports of where they played, or who was in the team. The first press reports in 1927 record the team in Herefordshire's *Section B*. They got off to a bad start with some heavy defeats, losing to Lydbrook 8-0, and to Tupsley in the cup 7-0 despite some heroics by the Fownhope goalie. However the team fortunes turned round – they held neighbours Holme Lacy to a draw, defeated Ewyas Harold 6-1, and turned the tables on Tupsley with a 2-0 win. The rare press reports only name one player – inside right Haines – and that's only because he was injured!

Why didn't the team continue? Was it because there was no recreation field – most of the team's early games were away matches – maybe because they had to wait for the last hay crop to get onto a farmer's field?

The Club re-formed at the New Inn in 1972. Amongst the driving forces were Les Gummery (publican at the New Inn), Islyn Davies, and trainer John Jones senior and wife Marjory who was secretary for many years. Later on Bill and John Davies and Dennis Harwood played a big part in the Club's success.

The team joined the *Herefordshire Sunday League* in autumn 1972 which required nets, marked lines, kit, insurance and changing facilities – a far cry, one suspects from the team of the 1920s.

Football team 1922                                    *M Dees*

Football matches were played from 1972 on Malthouse Field – the farmer Derek Williams set a limit of no more than two games per week, with no use before mid August and asked the club to avoid over-use in wet conditions. He charged no rent – instead the club helped him at hay-making! The teams changed in the (old) school.

Football team 1970s            *D Biggs*   Youth footballers 1970s            *D Biggs*

By 1975 there were three teams – the first team were promoted to the 1st division in 1978 and had a long run of success in cup and league – so much so that they were given the Shield to keep in 1986!

Among the stars was Paul Davies who scored over 100 goals in all competitions in 1983 and played in the NAYC cup final at Goodison Park. The team won the league and cup in 1991, when Jeremy Hope was voted player of the year. The club won six cup finals in the space of just 10 days in 1991!

They feature strongly in the centenary history of the League which records the final match of the 1999 season when a crowd of 300 watched Fownhope lose to old rivals Ewyas Harold – you can't win them all.

The Youth football team joined the *North Hereford Youth League* in 1972, reached the semi-finals of the county youth cup and swiftly became one of the best youth teams in Herefordshire. Several players joined the highly successful senior team in the *Herefordshire League.*

The Youth Club's golden era was in the early 1980s when they represented Herefordshire in the national youth clubs football competition. Fownhope reached the final in 1983 at Everton's Goodison Park (*one of the country's top grounds*) when they lost 3-1 to the Merseyside team drawn from a range of youth clubs. Fownhope's population? – *less than a thousand.* Merseyside's – *1,512,000!*

Football trophy                                         *J Jones*

## Brockhampton Cricket
Brockhampton's cricket team, now one of the best in the county, has had close links with Fownhope from it's formation in 1897. Several of the Fownhope

clergy have played for the team – from Frederick Nott to Gerald Bourdillon, Charles Cottrell and Claude Sell. Wilf Chignell played weekday games for the *'Herefordshire Gentlemen '* at Brockhampton. Arthur Ridler from Brick Cottage Oldstone was captain in 1958, when Claude Sell was second team vice-captain and later club secretary.

**NHS Trust**

**vs**

**The Lord's Taverners**

**CELEBRITY CRICKET MATCH**

**at**

**Fownhope,**

Cricket match                    *R Wargen*

By the 1980s the club was holding social events in Fownhope, and team names were posted in the village. A dozen Fownhope residents were amongst its players, including John Jones junior, Roy Wargen (captain 1990-3, chairman since 1992), and Michael Best (club captain 1987-91). Some third team games have been played on Fownhope's Recreation Field since the 1980s. The Lord's Taverners, included several test players and 'celebrities', in a charity match here against hospital doctors in August 1995.

**The Tennis Club** between 1933 and 1954 played on courts at the Vicarage and Bowens, and used the *Memorial Hall* for fund-raising and social events – dances and whist drives. The Club lapsed but the village is well served by a club in Woolhope.

**The Badminton Club** played in the old Memorial Hall from 1947 *(their first recorded booking)* to 1955, and re-appeared in 1970. Geoffrey Hardwick was involved. However it must have lapsed because a new Club *(no records of their predecessors)* was formed when the new Hall opened in 1987. The new club currently had 14 members in 2007 and plays for fun once a week.

# THE COUNTRYSIDE

Much of the Parish Council's time was taken up in the 1920s and 1930s in ensuring that the historic network of footpaths, recorded on the first detailed *Ordnance Survey* map in 1887, was kept open. The Parish Council, led by Wilf Chignell, Godfrey Malkin, and Vera Biggs later worked with local farmers to recorded these paths on the '*Definitive Map*' produced by the County Council in 1956, and revised again in 1989. Hiking was a popular pastime and local footpaths were well used in the 1950s as they have continued to be.

When the Act came into existence we took it very seriously. Vera Biggs and I, with one or two of the other more mobile members of the Parish Council, walked miles of footpaths … they were all marked on maps and sent to the County Council who had to see they were kept open and in reasonable order … quite a number of paths were questioned … and a public meeting held before an arbitrator appointed by the Government. We won nearly all of them.

*Memoirs of Rev Wilf Chignell, Vicar 1948-56*

HNT at Common Hill                                           *S Gough*

The *National Trust* acquired a strip of Haugh Wood called Poors Acre in 1931. The *Herefordshire Nature Trust* acquired Rudge End Quarry in 1972, followed by Nupend in 1973, Lea and Paget Wood in 1977, and Monument Hill and the old Cider House in 1984. These areas are managed as wildlife reserves. *English Nature*, designated these, as well as Cherry Hill, Haugh Wood, Capler Wood, and the River Wye between 1983 and 1996 as '*Sites of Special Scientific Interest*'. The *Forestry Commission* opened up Haugh Wood in the 1980s to walkers and cyclists, whilst also giving more attention to wildlife.

169

I used to love doing the round during the spring. to go through Lea Wood was absolutely heaven. Bluebells, primroses, the harebells, it was really beautiful and Common Hill too – lots of violets, and cowslips.

*Dora Grant, with Mandy Dees & Pam Colley, 2006*

The parish was included in the *Wye Valley Area of Outstanding Natural Beauty* in 1971. The Wye Valley Walk, a long distance footpath was signed through the parish in 1990 from Capler Farm by Common Hill to Mordiford. Some 3,600 walkers per year were recorded on the way in the parish by2005. The *British Horse Society* held national championships in Haugh Wood in 2000. This was followed by a national orienteering event – though there were complaints that some paths were overgrown!

Baynams alley                    *D M Clark*

The Parish Council appointed a volunteer footpath officer in 1997 to report problems. David Clarke took on the role in 1999 and helped the *Residents Association* produce a series of leaflets and guided walks. The Medical Centre joined them to start a series of health walks which developed into a regular walks programme.

Fownhope and Holme Lacy Parish Councils promoted a new Millenium footbridge to replace the lost ferry crossing, an idea first mooted in 1897 Detailed proposals were made by a committee chaired by Derek Colley, backed by a parish poll, but the County Council felt unable to proceed without the agreement of one of the landowners affected.

170

# PARISH COUNCIL

The Parish Council, set up in 1894, had taken over the civil duties of the Vestry. Ten councillors were elected by show of hands for a three year term at a meeting of voters in the School. There were 15 candidates for 10 places in 1919 but by 1928 the elections went uncontested.

---

### Chairmen

| | |
|---|---|
| Dr Edgar A Jones 1897-1919 | Desmond J Biggs 1980 & 1996-99 |
| John Griffiths 1919 -20 | Margaret E Biggs 1982 |
| Edmund F Gange 1920-23 | Malcolm Hillier 1984 |
| Capel J Hardwick 1923-35 | Austin J Seely 1985 |
| Arthur Powell 1935-41 | Kenneth Turner 1988 |
| Harry Lloyd 1941-46 | George Sharman 1989 |
| Rev Edwin D Preston 1946-7 | Richard H Garnett 1986 & 1990-2 |
| Dr Godfrey Malkin 1947-65 | Margaret Mason 1992-4 |
| John R Crowe 1966 | George Thomas 1994-6 |
| Dr Patrick Ramage 1967-77 & 1979, | John Hardwick 2000-4 |
| 1981, 1983 & 1987 | John TW Jones 2004-7 |
| Cecil Prosser 1977-79 | Martin Williams 2007 |

### Clerks

| | |
|---|---|
| | Arthur B Clements 1969-72 |
| Frederick Jones 1894-1932 | Margaret E Biggs 1972-77 |
| George L Biggs 1932-45 | Vera M Biggs 1977-78 |
| Fred Probyn 1945 | Ann E Brown 1978-88 |
| Alfred C Leney 1946-52 | Christopher Whitmey 1988-95 |
| Molly Haines 1952-61 | Lynda P Willcox 1995-2005 |
| Dora Grant 1962-69 | Keith Shilton 2006-7 |

---

The Council has always had several farmers and local trades people. There were no women members in the 1920s, though they had been eligible since 1894. The WI encouraged members to stand. Three women were elected in 1946 though there have only two women chairmen in 113 years.

---

### Parish Councillors 1946

| | | |
|---|---|---|
| Godfrey Malkin | Mona | Doctor |
| Harry Fagg | Green Man | Publican |
| John Pritchard | Walworth House | Butcher |
| Ruth Biggs | Canon House | |
| Florence St Barbe | Whiterdine | retired |
| Stanley Hardwick | Oldstone | Farmer |
| Alfred Chamberlain | Orchard Lodge | Gardener/fireman |
| Beryl Duncombe | Orchard Cottage | Retired |
| Lewis Haines | Common Hill | Farm worker |
| Dick Biggs | Lechmere Ley | farmer |

Bylaws

School

Secret ballot was introduced for the 1947 elections. There were 12 candidates for the 10 seats in 1949, with the doctor topping the poll, followed closely by Harry Fagg, the retiring publican at the Green Man, the new vicar, Mervyn Davies the farmer at Mill Farm and Alf Leney, the postmaster. The council met quarterly in the 1920s and spent much of its time discussing the state of the wells, pumps and footpaths and acting as the voice of the village.

Capel Hardwick, farmer at Oldstone, Arthur Powell timber merchant from Lucksall and Harry Lloyd shopkeeper at West End Stores held the post of chairman in the 23 years between 1923 and 1946. They were soon followed by Godfrey Malkin who served for 18 years, to be followed by another doctor, Patrick Ramage, who held the chair 14 times. Since 1977 few people have served as chairman for more than two years. Three generations of Hardwick and Powell have served on the Council. Patrick Ramage produced typed reports for meetings in the 1970s when standing orders and committees were introduced to assist council business.

Fred Jones from Highland Place was clerk for 38 years, combining the work with that of rates and tax collector. He was unpaid but his successor George Biggs, was paid £2 10s in 1932. Alf Leney, postmaster, was paid £4 in 1945, and the stipend had risen to £25 in 1969 when Dora Grant retired. Clerks have been active local residents. However since 1995 both clerks have lived elsewhere, serving several other parish councils.

The Council, along with the district and county councils, raised money from every ratepayer in the parish. The precept stayed at £10 through the 1930s, was £30 by 1964, but has steadily risen, to £200 in 1972, £1289 in 1975, £8900 in 1996, and £16,000 in 2003.

Old school conversion                                    *D M Clark*

The annual **Parish Meeting** has provided everybody with a chance to have their say. Attendances were rarely large unless there was a burning issue. The 1949 meeting attracted 71 people to talk about housing developments and street lighting but a year later only 11 attended. The meeting in 1958 drew a few councillors but no members of the public, and numbers rarely reached double figures until the 1980s when Patrick Ramage went to great lengths to overcome the apathy. Even then the debate about a new hall only drew 86 people in 1984, compared with the 386 who had voted in the ballot.

Acting as the village voice could bring the Council into conflict with other powers. Relations with the Rural District Council were often strained, notably over water supplies and housing development. At one point the parish was so critical of the RDC that the RDC had to pass a motion of confidence in their Clerk. Another dispute prompted the Parish to seek a move to another RDC area!

The Council has campaigned on many issues dealt with elsewhere in this book – on postal services, mains water, sewerage, footpaths, roads, library service, lighting, phones, fire station and power supplies. They have commented on planning applications since 1974. The Council has also taken on direct responsibility for some services, e.g. the squash courts in the Old School, acquired the recreation field, supported the loan for the new Hall, and planted trees.

# POLICING

Fownhope's constables had been elected, albeit with some reluctance, for 300 years before paid professionals took over in the late 19th century. The village had a resident bobby based at the Police Station in Fern Cottage.

| Resident Constables | |
|---|---|
| at Fern Cottage | Sam Painter 1921-9,  Edwin Everett 1932-44, Alf Mangham 1946-8  Phil Paton 1952-3 |
| 17 Court Orchard | Phil Paton 1953-8, Alf Cousins 1958-68, David Parker 1968-74 |

Fern Cottage                                    *M Best*

PC Everett                                    *M Best*

There are very few press reports of serious crime – a stray pig in 1921, a theft of gloves, a neighbour dispute at Nupend, driving without a license in 1936, and cycling without lights in 1939. However the police constable's very presence may have been sufficient deterrent.

---

**FOWNHOPE ROWDYISM THREE YOUTHS FINED**

Three youths summoned for being drunk and disorderly at Fownhope. PC Painter returning to his station at midnight on Sunday … saw 12 to 15 fellows standing by the Post Office, singing '*Ukelele Lady*' shouting, and using foul language … nothing unusual for them to have a jar of cider with them after closing hours … defendants called at the Green Man after church, (stayed) till closing time at 10 o'clock. Harold Monkley, grocer, heard one say *"Oh here is PC Painter. We do not care for him."* George Thomas, blacksmith, also gave evidence.

*two were from 'dry' Holme Lacy! Hereford Times, Oct 1927*

---

Crime was on the increase in the post-war years but it seems to have largely escaped Fownhope. Harold Green was found not guilty of stealing two rabbits at Mordiford. There was a break-in at the New Inn in 1949, and more serious events next door:

Thomas Rathbone charged with stealing a shirt and two collars of the value of £2, the property of Mr Joseph Nicholls, and the woman who has since become his wife Pamela charged with stealing one pair of cami-knickers, and two silver hip flasks, the property of Mrs Grace Nicholls of the value of £13. Prosecuting, Supt F Wheatley said the defendants went to the Green Man Inn at 9 p.m., and signed the register as Dr and Mrs Lawson. It was discovered the bed had not been slept in and the articles named were missing. Rathbone said that he had been in prison for the past three months and that it had taught him a lesson. Mr J Whinnie, appearing for Mrs Rathbone, said the two young people had run away from home and had visited a number of cities throughout the country. Rathbone was conditionally discharged and his wife was granted an absolute discharge.

*Hereford Times March 1952*

Phil Paton took over from Arthur Deakin in 1952.

We covered as far as Ballingham and Dormington. I got about on my pedal cycle, was paid an allowance of 1s 6d a week, plus torch of 6d

A policeman in the country was on duty 24 hours of the day – four hours in the morning, four in the evening, probably travel 20 miles per shift on bike

We used to have one or two silly youngsters go and break windows up at Fownhope Court which was derelict for many years. I'd go to see the youngsters with their parents – *"you've got 7 days to replace the window or you'll be prosecuted."* – the window was always repaired.

Nobody ever got prosecuted for poaching though you did have poaching. Fownhope families were all related to one and another … you had to be careful who you were talking to! My wife Olive was very much an unpaid policewoman – people would ring up to talk to the local bobby.

*Phil Paton, PC here 1952-58, talking to Pam Colley & Madge Daines, 2006*

The county proposed to close the station in 1970, and cease to have a resident constable. The parish council objected but the office had moved to Bartestree by 1974. The parish council helped to set up a neighbourhood watch scheme in the 1990s but this too has lapsed.

# THE WEATHER

The vicar, Thomas West, had found time to man a weather station at the Vicarage in the 1890s. This was continued in the 1920s by Frances Cresswell at Lowerhouse and Morney Cross. There were notable floods in 1925 and 1927, and severe cold in 1927 and 1929.

1947 snow          *N Cope*   Floods Ferry Lane                          *J Soulsby*

*... river flooding gave us worry after going out with the pony and trap at 3 a.m. to rescue poultry on two occasions. One flood almost reached the incubator – we lost cut hay and cider apples in autumn floods.*

*Helena R Biggs at Lechmere Ley in 1930s*

River frozen 1963          *G Powell*   Common Hill snow 1973          *J Soulsby*

Few will ever forget the winter of 1947. Godfrey Malkin recorded that the snow lay for 50 days from 24th January till 23rd March. Coal was in short supply, and there were power cuts. The roads were extremely difficult. The chains slipped off Godfrey Malkin's *Rover*, and he had to complete some visits on foot, or rely on Matthew Leyman's jeep to get through 15" of snow to Old Sufton. No buses ran to Hereford. The Ross snow plough did not reach Fownhope. The snow was followed by heavy rain, and a rapid thaw which led to flooding. The hot summer was some consolation. Eleanor Pugh's log book records some of the challenges: 1947 –

## The Winter Of '47- School Log Book

| | |
|---|---|
| *7 Jan* | school reopened … very bad weather |
| *26 Jan* | school had to be closed … very cold weather, low attendance 19/41 and fuel shortage.  School is open for milk & meals |
| *24 Feb* | school closed owing to lack of fuel … deep snows, floods and no transport for school fuel … school meals and milk have been served on all days with three exceptions |
| *21 March* | school re-opened today |

Snow above Leabring 1973?                                    *J Soulsby*

Mary Soulsby recorded the great freeze of 1963 in her diary:

*Jan 1*   Thick layer of snow fell overnight Woolhope, Ross cut off

*Jan 3*   No bus after 5.50pm from Hereford

*Jan 8*   Ross bus did get up the Nash for the first time

*Jan 12*  Minimum 7°F (-14°C) – milk didn't arrive until late evening – frozen cream

*Jan 14*  School not back – chemical closets frozen

*Jan 23*  Colder than ever – silver rime over the trees

*Jan 25*  Water frozen at the mains … boys carrying water.  Wont be able to do the washing

*Feb 3*   Council sent water tanker to fill up tanks

*Mar 3*   John went a walk up the Nash.  Snow drifts as high as myself

*Mar 6*   Ice and snow melting rapidly great ice floes down the river – river well over road at Mordiford.

There were more floods in December 1964, 1976 1990, and again in 1998, recorded by Denzil Biggs and Sue Clifford.

Floods below Rock Ho                *J Soulsby*    Floods by Holme Lacy            *J Soulsby*

Floods 1998                         *S Clifford*    Floods 1998                     *S Clifford*

Floods Tanhouse 1998                *D Biggs*       Tanhouse floods                 *S Clifford*

# FOWNHOPE's FUTURE?

Fownhope has witnessed many changes since 1919. We now enjoy mains water supply, sewerage, electricity, gas and a bus service. We have an excellent new Hall, sports field and leisure centre and a 'new' school has replaced the old. We have a much enhanced medical facility and have kept our resident clergyman. We have kept a range of shops, pubs and other services, and there are more jobs locally than in 1919, albeit much changed. We have a wide range of clubs and activities reported in a lively new monthly magazine. There is still a sense of community, well reflected in the annual *Club Walk* day. And the countryside may have changed with modern farming, but it remains a source of pleasure and relaxation.

Success inevitably comes with some costs. Many residents bemoan the increase in traffic, particularly on the main road, and regret the cuts in the bus service. Many homes are empty through the day as their occupiers commute long distances to work, passing others travelling to work in the village!. We cannot take our local services for granted – we must *'use it or lose it'*. New building in the past 50 years has ensured a better balance of housing stock than in most Herefordshire villages but many council homes have been sold off without assurances that they will remain in local hands. House prices, in common with much of rural England, are beyond the reach of many would-be first-time buyers.

The planners, instructed to find sites for new housing, may be tempted to stretch the village 'envelope'. Fownhope's current success is based in part on the scale of development that has taken place in the past half century. Would more development bring better services? Or would it spoil the village's character and setting? There is plenty of scope for a lively debate within this articulate community. Sadly decisions on this, and others that directly affect us, will be decided by outside bodies over which we have little effective control. What a contrast with the days when Fownhope was responsible for its own schooling, highways, policing and social security! But that's a story for another book.

# INDEX OF PEOPLE & FAMILIES